"Whew child, if I'd had this book in my 20s, I would have been a millionaire many times over by now! This book is a must-read, especially for women entering the workforce. Building wealth is really as simple as Saving 10!" —**Naseema McElroy, founder of Financially Intentional and host of *Nurses on Fire* podcast**

"Our family of four designed a 'work-optional' life by the time I was 39. We had median incomes as a nurse and chef with two little girls and live in a high-cost-of-living area, so people often ask how we did it. Sarah-Catherine Gutierrez's book brilliantly summarizes the core concepts that were part of our journey, and I'm so thrilled to recommend it to others who would like to design a life as we have. So often, people want to learn about how we invested, but it is essential to learn the core concepts of money management and savings first, otherwise it is the equivalent of remodeling your kitchen when your garage is on fire. This book is a road map to design a life of time freedom that is simply priceless. Crafting this life *is* possible and it all begins with the plan to Save 10." —**Lynn Frair, founder of fihealthcare.com**

"This book is a game changer for anyone who doesn't understand the life-changing benefits of paying themselves first—or how to go about doing it. *But First, Save 10* has demystified the financial concepts necessary for long-term financial success. Every woman should read this book to help equip them to not only take control of their finances, but also help get them closer to living their ideal life: one filled with financial freedom." —**B.C. Krygowski, MD, FIRE (Financial Independence Retire Early) blogger, hospice and palliative medicine physician**

"Women have advantages and disadvantages when it comes to earning, saving, investing, spending, and giving wisely. This is the book that will teach them to maximize the advantages while minimizing the disadvantages en route to financial freedom. It will make a wonderful graduation gift for my daughters and nieces." —**James M. Dahle, MD, FACEP, founder of The White Coat Investor, author of** *The White Coat Investor: A Doctor's Guide to Personal Finance and Investing*

"This should be required reading for college grads. In a world hell-bent on telling us to spend, spend, spend, we need more voices like Gutierrez's, encouraging us to save, save, save. When I was younger, I believed that my financial freedom was dependent on making a high income. Then, I started making a high income, and realized that the habit of saving and investing early would have been much more powerful. Saving can be difficult because most of us only realize its value after we've gotten ourselves into financial messes. Gutierrez's approach in reaching people before they ever cause themselves financial pain is brilliant. Her guidance is simple and empowering." —**Diania Merriam, Chief EconoMeist, EconoMe Conference**

"Every teen and young adult should read this book before making any major financial decisions in their lives. Sarah-Catherine Gutierrez does an amazing job of reaching young women exactly where they are and breaking down seemingly complex financial topics into approachable action steps that will help any reader conquer their finances. This book can take a young adult who is blissfully unaware of how important their finances are and transform them into a supercharged, wealth-building state of mind."
—**Rob Phelan, ChooseFI Personal Finance Curriculum Developer, author of** *The Simple StartUp: A Beginner's Guide To Starting A Business*, **and high school personal finance teacher**

"As a father of two young girls—and a self-proclaimed money nerd—Sarah-Catherine Gutierrez's book *But First, Save 10* is the EXACT book I want my daughters to read to learn about personal finance. It is empowering, uplifting, and full of relatable (and humorous) examples. It is a testament to Gutierrez's passion and purpose to help young women everywhere recognize that they have the power to take control of their lives, but first they must (and should) read this book!" —**Jimmy Turner, MD, anesthesiologist, author of** *The Physician Philosopher's Guide to Personal Finance*, **and host of the** *Money Meets Medicine* **podcast**

"One of the most important acts of self-sufficiency is having a healthy relationship with money. This is especially true for women who have historically been on the wrong side of a money-power dynamic. In *But First, Save 10*, Sarah-Catherine Gutierrez offers invaluable advice on how we can take control of our finances in a way that is productive and empowering. I believe taking the steps in her book will give women the impetus to fully realize their worth and ask for what they're worth. Advocates like Gutierrez are the teachers we need, and her book is a vital step in achieving true financial health." —**Georgia Pellegrini, host of** *Modern Pioneering* **(PBS) and** *Wild Food* **(Discovery), author of** *Modern Pioneering: More Than 150 Recipes, Projects, and Skills for a Self-Sufficient Life; Girl Hunter: Revolutionizing the Way We Eat, One Hunt at a Time;* **and** *Food Heroes: Sixteen Culinary Artisans Preserving Tradition*

"Sarah-Catherine Gutierrez is one of the nicest 'forces of nature' you will ever meet. When she turned her attention to 'money,' she set her sights on *SAVING*, an old fashioned, quaint, and nearly outdated financial concept. She then selected young women, a group rarely selected by the financial industry, as her target audience. The result, *But First, Save 10*, is concise, clever, and laugh-out-loud funny in places. Reading it is a seismic experience. Your view of money will change, your life will change, and it will all be for the better and for the long term. Enjoy."
—**Linda Bessette, author of** *Mindful Money: A Path to Simple Finances*

BUT FIRST, SAVE 10

The One Simple Money Move That Will Change Your Life

ladysplaining
MONEY

SARAH-CATHERINE GUTIERREZ

Yours in Havery
SCG

To my darling Jorge, keeper of love, truth, and integrity.

CONTENTS

Introduction xi

Spender or Saver: How Will You Write Your Life Story? 1

The Inspiration: Pay Yourself First and Save 10 11
    Book Roadmap
    This is Not About Investing
    Compound Interest Chart

The Perspiration 23

Women Will Lead Us Out of This Savings Crisis 27
    Build Your Cash Pile Now: Not Piling = Not an Option
    Know Better, Do Better
    Don't Waste Brain Power Worrying About Investing
    (Even Though Women Are Pretty Good at It)
        But First, Save
        Closing Gender Disparities
        Save10 Could Save Us All

The Financial Industry 49
    Selling and Advising Should Not Be Confused
    Fee-Only Advice is Less Conflicted Advice, But Still . . .
    Fixed-Fee Advising is the Next Advancement

Retirement Dream to Retirement Reality 59

Step 1: Pay Yourself First 63

How Much Should Olivia Save?

What is the Company's Match or Contribution?

Vesting Schedule

You Can't Beat the Tax Benefit of This Plan Combined with Automation

    Roth 401(k), 403(b), and 457(b)

    Pre-Tax, or Traditional 401(k), 403(b), or 457(b)

Saving for Retirement When You Have Credit Card Debt

Saving for Retirement When You Have Student Loan Debt

Saving for Retirement When You Get Pay Increases

Never Ever Ever Ever Ever Cash Out

Don't Have a Retirement Plan?

Start your Emergency Fund While You Are Saving

Tell the World You're a Saver

Invest Your Savings 101

Bucking the Intimidation of Jargon

    Stocks

    Bonds

    Mutual Funds

Passive Index Funds

Use Target Date Retirement Funds

Recap: How to Invest

Start Your Emergency Fund

Step 2: Pay for Future Expenses 121

Dream Saving is Inspiring

Why Separate, Named Savings Accounts?

Choosing Your Accounts

Emergency Fund

Travel

Weddings and Baby Showers

Health Savings Accounts (HSAs)

    Healthcare Survival

    HSA as a Retirement Account

Gifts

Technology

Cars

Insurance

Clothes and "Beauty"

Homes

    Home Repair Savings

Kids: College Saving and Summer Activities

Making it Work

Step 3: Pay Your Bills |7|

    Reduce or Eliminate Bills

    Pay Your Bills

Step 4: Spend the Rest |85

    How to Spend the Rest

    Gamification

    Marriage Saver

    Why a Debit Card for Step 4?

    How Should You Build Your Credit?

The Big Picture 203

    The System

    Reconciling Accounts Each Month

    Olivia's New Financial Path

    He Said "Yes" (to The System)

You Can Do This 225

You're Invited to Join the Save10 Movement 229

Sources, Resources, & Tools 231

Acknowledgments 239

Retirement Dreams 245

INTRODUCTION

Will you become a saver or a spender?

Many (perhaps most) women look back on their working lives and realize that their paycheck was used to pay many others, through taxes to the government, premiums to the insurance company, fees to the parking garage, and the automatic draft to the gym. The hard-earned net paycheck then went to housing payments, car payments, monthly subscriptions, cell phone payments, and the like. All that money was paid to other people with the hope or expectation that maybe some would be left over, that perhaps some could be saved after everyone got paid. But month after month, year after year, pay raise after pay raise, nothing ever made it through the funnel. After decades, these hard working people wake up to discover that despite so many years of trying to do everything right, there is nothing left for freedom and flexibility, little left for retirement.

In the end, will you have to live with the realization that everyone got paid out of your paycheck except you? Or instead, might you consider setting a different course for yourself by paying yourself first? You may already have your answer or you may still need convincing. Either way, this book is your why and how.

As I'm writing this introduction, it is the spring of 2020, and we're in the midst of a global pandemic. On a cataclysmic scale, it is changing everything—from the world economy to our personal lives. It is transforming what we took for granted just months before. While it seems like the virus's spread is halting practically every part of our lives, if we look closely, it is also offering us an opportunity that we rarely have glaring at us in such rich technicolor.

Let's step outside of ourselves for a moment and into a fortune teller's booth, where she shows us this global pandemic from an imaginary distance. Her crystal ball offers a glimpse of the events that we are experiencing now as well as a possible future. Many people lost their jobs, their homes, and their ability to put food on the table. Most lived in fear of mortal danger for themselves and those they loved. They couldn't stop reading the news to reveal the next calamity and couldn't stop checking their plummeting 401(k) numbers. Some people, the lucky ones, got paid to stay home and work, even though not much work was happening. On one hand, it felt like doom, but at the same time, certain parts of life began to change for the better. They didn't have to set an alarm clock. The morning sprint was replaced by a lingering cup of coffee, sipped while gazing at the birds, whose feathers and habits they learned by heart. They planted that garden they'd always wanted to start. They read books. They called up that friend they hadn't spoken to in years. They dusted off the sewing machine and made masks for frontline workers. They heard a voice inside that said slowing down and working toward the common good *felt* good, and they vowed to take the good parts with them, come what may.

The fortune teller's hand shifts and points to the future, a world in which the unprecedented social distancing is over and people emerge once more. They are called back in to work—back to the normal schedule. Only this time, they remember how it felt to be awash in those good feelings, and they don't want to go back to normal. Suddenly awakened to the value and beauty of this one life they have to live and panicked by the notion that it could be ripped away, by outside forces totally beyond their control, they vow to do what *is* in their control—they slash expenses, pay down student loan debt, don't buy houses they'd considered, find realtors to help them get their oversized homes on the market, and downsize their luxury cars. They take years off to finally clinch their dreams to write books, launch tech startups, or start bakeries. Deep within their bones, the people now know that nothing, no material possession, is worth trading something far more important—their time.

The crystal ball goes dark, but I hope you'll allow the impression to remain.

We are in the middle of this terrible, extraordinary moment, and there's no predicting what will happen, but this pandemic could be the catalyst that changes the generational rhythm, the seismic shift that leads countless among us to jump off the hedonic treadmill and walk toward designing our own lives instead. What if all it takes to step into that dream is dipping into our courage and starting a pile of cash?

In fact, what if you decide now never to hop on the treadmill in the first place? What if you emerge through your 20s with education and training to discover that your real source of power is the pile of cash that enables you to put your education and training to work as you pursue your deepest life dreams? If Jason Zweig is right, and I think he is, "[i]n the end, living a rich life depends less on how much you own than on how much you do, what you stand for, and how fully you reach your own potential."[1] A pile of cash gives you the freedom of choice, the freedom to walk away, the freedom to live life on your own terms. Or, as JL Collins so simply describes it, "Money can buy many things, but nothing more valuable than your freedom."[2]

So I'll ask again: Will you become a saver or a spender?

SPENDER OR SAVER: HOW WILL YOU WRITE YOUR LIFE STORY?

"While money has no intrinsic reality, our life energy does—at least to us
. . . . It is precious because it is limited and irretrievable and because our
choices about how we use it express the meaning and purpose of our time
here on earth."   — Vicki Robin[3]

I want you to become a saver. Right now. You've already taken the first
step by opening this book. Maybe you feel responsible, hopeful, or even
excited. Remember this feeling, because the journey of being a saver
will likely bring just as much satisfaction as the moment you wake up
with your first $1,000 saved, and continue with your first $10,000 and
$100,000. Do these numbers sound big? We're about to make them
possible, even probable, and thoroughly enjoy ourselves while we do it.
In *The Happiness Hypothesis,* Jonathan Haidt says, "Set for yourself any
goal you want. Most of the pleasure will be had along the way . . . The
final moment of success is often no more thrilling than the relief of
taking off a heavy backpack at the end of a long hike."[4]

To demonstrate the pleasure that is possible and more deeply teach
these concepts, we are going to walk the journey of a woman named
Olivia. She is a composite character, representative of many young
people I have spoken with about their money in my role as financial

advisor and also reflective of statistical averages for women in her age group. If she is not representative of you, that's entirely okay. Please don't let those wonderful differences keep you from learning from her. By applying the book's concepts to Olivia's life, you will be better able to apply them to your own.

Now, meet Olivia. This 23-year-old graduates college with $50,000 in student loan debt, gets an exciting new job making $45,000, and then moves back in with her parents to pay off that debt, only to find herself neck-deep in credit cards from two large graduation trips and a shopping spree for work clothes. Don't forget the brand new, hip Subaru, the car of her dreams. She takes on a $500 car payment co-signed by her parents at 12% interest. She makes these decisions knowing she is about to make more money than she has ever had in her life.

When her paycheck arrives, it doesn't amount to nearly as much as she imagined. She panics, hoping it will somehow be better next month. But it isn't.

After all those credit card and car payments, there isn't much left. Olivia is wondering how she will pay the student loan payments when the grace period ends in a few months. It is apparent that she will never be able to get her own apartment. And, no, she has not signed up for the company retirement plan, wondering, *How am I supposed to think about saving for retirement in my 20s when I have student loans and a car payment?* Alarmed by her situation, too embarrassed to tell her parents or friends, she goes online to sell her car. Then, she discovers that what she can get for it is less than what she signed up to pay. The car is underwater. To walk away would cost $7,000 out of pocket.

Olivia is 23 and broke and seems to be sentenced to being broke for a long time. She is sad, scared, and stressed. She is ashamed. The hope she felt while walking across the stage at her college graduation has vanished.

Growing up, no one sat down with Olivia to discuss money. Her parents bought her nice things, which she was grateful for. But they never explained *how* they bought things large or small for themselves, *how* they afforded them, nor *how much* (if any) they had in retirement. Somehow, Olivia absorbed the message that she wasn't supposed to ask. When she took on the student loan debt, no one explained to her what it would mean, what kind of sacrifice she would have to make for her future self to afford it; she understood only what she would gain from the loan, not what she would lose.

Let's break it down. The only thing she was ever taught in life was consumption. Not saving. As Vicki Robin describes our modern relationship to money, "We project onto money the capacity to fulfill our fantasies, allay our fears, soothe our pain." Rather than living life, she makes the case that "we consume it."[5] Can someone explain to me why we judge Olivia for doing the very things we taught her to do? For consuming. For being in so much debt. For not saving.

We know Olivia knows what saving is and probably agrees that saving is a good idea. But the condition she has started her life in would be akin to learning in a one-hour lesson in high school about programming and then being expected to work as a computer programmer after graduating college with an English degree.

The news loves to report this story. It's a narrative that the older generations can read and then shake their heads in disapproval, momentarily disrupted when it's their turn in the Starbucks line to order a venti, nonfat, extra hot latte.

Let's put the judgement hat on. Olivia:

1. Is Gen Z/Millennial
2. Lives at home
3. Spends without an understanding of budget
4. Has a high-interest car loan
5. Has too much student loan debt

Olivia's story is real, but for every extreme story like hers, there are 10 more that are less severe, equally heartbreaking, and sadly common. I find most people are breaking even (no debt but no savings) or undersaving to the point that retirement will not be an enjoyable experience.

In recent decades, we graduate from high school and, often, college into a harsh world. It is a world where we receive credit cards in our mailboxes on a weekly basis, encouraging us to spend. We might even get checks with those cards. Want a car? No problem. Who pays cash for their cars anymore? "No one."

You likely grew up in a household where your only observance of money was your parents' spending. You have been and continue to be encouraged, cheered on even, to spend, spend, spend. But then, at some point, reality sets in. Those minimum credit card payments that used to be $10 are suddenly a lot higher. You realize that the total owed on all those cards is a big number, too big to know how you would ever pay them off. Making that car payment is much more difficult than you had calculated in your head—certainly more than the car salesperson made it sound to be.

You are stressed. And this is not like cramming-for-exams stressed. Remember those few days before the test when you feel like you will never get there? You can't possibly get through the book that you never read. You are surely going to fail. But then you take the test. You don't fail, and you sleep for three weeks on your parents' couch at the end of the semester, emerging a new you.

Financial stress? This is a different kind of stress. It's the kind that is always there. Dinner with friends after work? It's there when you order your entrée, when the check arrives, when the friend mentions the promotion that you desperately need for a pay raise. It's there when you go on vacation (on credit) to get away from the stress. But you feel the stress constantly in the pit of your stomach. *Sure this vacation is nice, but how can I afford the payments when I get back to the grind?* It's there when your best friend is getting married, and instead of being excited during the ceremony, you are just hoping there will be enough money in your account on Friday, payday, to Venmo the bride for your bridesmaid dress.

Maybe none of this resonates with you. You would never buy a new car, after all. You understand the pitfalls of credit cards. But is it possible that your financial challenge could be something different? Maybe it's the nicer apartment that you justify getting because it would allow you to walk to work. Maybe you eat out a lot because it makes sense to network on the job. Maybe your health is important to you so you spend hundreds on a gym membership and expensive supplements. Maybe beauty is important to you so you spend hundreds on skin care and expensive haircuts, manicures, and pedicures.

Most people are walking around, trapped in their own justifications of spending. They are spenders convincing themselves they are savers (or would-be savers) if only they made more money, didn't have to fix their cars, didn't need an expensive medical procedure, etc., etc., etc. They curiously look at other forms of spending as frivolous but somehow don't see their own. And the stories are typically not as severe as the first situation. Usually, the stories are the big life coincidences—that everything people bring home in their take-home pay seems to be just the right amount that they need, count on, rely on, couldn't manage to survive without.

What if I told you this inability to save is largely attributed to the wiring of our human brains? In the history of the human race, people didn't have to save for retirement because there was no such thing. They died during working years. But we can't plan to work throughout our entire lives, whether by choice or because our health gives out on us. As Jonathan Clements points out, "America's miserably low savings rate partly stems from our short-term focus. But it also reflects our lack of self-control. Our ancestors didn't have to worry about restraining their consumption so they could amass money for retirement. We, alas, do need self-control. But for most of us, it is a lifelong struggle."[6]

Our ancestors didn't need retirement, but they also didn't have credit available to them. If they wanted something they didn't have, they had to pay or trade for it. So now we have this double whammy—the hunter-gatherer complex that dominates the brain to feed us for today and the credit cards that only work to reinforce, rather than tame, that influence.

Do not be dismayed. We can fix this. But we have to do some brain work. Pronto.

You have to *want* to save, and I don't take for granted that you do. It was not always my priority in life. In every single case I witness of a young person in the pain of living beyond their means, I have also clearly seen the alternative path that could have resulted in that same young person sitting in front of me with joy. The joy of missing out on the consumption train (JOMO) is the opposite of the fear of missing out (FOMO), which financially comes to represent the things we buy, from physical things to experiences, because our neighbors or friends are buying them. In fact, in many cases, we discussed the alternative path and how they wish they had taken it.

> **JOMO**
>
> The opposite of the Fear of Missing Out (FOMO). The joy of knowing what it is like to have savings in retirement, money in a savings account, and absolutely no debt.

The difference, really, is how quickly I can get in front of someone before they have made major life mistakes on debt. If I can catch them before renting the apartment, before buying the car, before setting the lifestyle, they will probably take that narrow, obscure path of financial freedom and start saving. It is that easy. Those early wins rewire the brain. The small financial wins become bigger ones over time.

My approach to helping people save in a large-scale way is to get in front of them on their first day at a company as the advisor to retirement plans. My colleagues and I get to have a half-hour conversation with an employee to try and convince them to save. It often works well, particularly for people starting out in life or who don't have high fixed expenses. We ask them to save, and then they do. If it is this simple, and I know that it works, how can we reach people beyond the scope of the retirement plans we serve?

Hence this book. It is my way to get behind the megaphone and reach more of you with the life-changing money moves I have seen work again and again. It is your roadmap to start out life avoiding, or re-start your life after, financial pain.

Have you answered the question yet? Are you a saver or a spender? Maybe you knee-jerk responded "saver" (yay!), but after reading on, realized that you are probably at risk of being a spender. Our natural habitat is consumption and debt. To be a saver is, in many ways, counter-cultural or abnormal. If you read this book and follow the plan to design your life and budget, you will become a saver. And when you start early enough, you only have to save a relatively small amount to live the life of your own design. It's when you start later that saving becomes more difficult, more painful.

> **Lifestyle Creep**
>
> The incremental purchases, subscriptions, or payments that we continue to take on as long as there is money in the bank.

I believe that financial pain does not have to be a rite of passage. We are going to end this, you and me. Together, we will fend off lifestyle creep. Legend has it that John D. Rockefeller was asked by a reporter how much money was enough. He is rumored to have responded, "Just a little bit more."

I am going to make you a saver by the time we finish this book. Perhaps this sounds exciting. Or maybe, a little frightening. The great news? If you start now, it is not nearly as tough as you might think. There is one time in your life that saving will be easy for you: right now. Not in six months, not when you make more money. Right now.

Saving

A rare condition wherein a person spends less than they make, diagnosed in the post- World War II era, but mostly eradicated in the subsequent generations.

When you are in your 20s, there is a line out the door of older adults telling you what to do. My goal here is not to tell you what to do, rather to illuminate the financial path that offers happiness. I am going to prove the point that the path of saving will make you happier.

One of the words in the industry, "finance," goes in through the ears and sets the eyes aglaze. For some reason, finance seems to be conflated with investing. Investments are great, and I want you to benefit from growing your savings over time through investing. But the investing industry of-

Finance

Paying for stuff with your money or other people's money (debt).

ten is dominated by people whose high comes from calculating stock valuations and whose fears are triggered by inverted yield curves. They get misty-eyed when recalling the moment, on that gorgeous fall day, when they first learned to read the stock ticker symbols in the paper. If you have no idea what I just said, I can tell you with authority that you can live your life not knowing or understanding it. Yes, there are basic concepts of investing you need to understand, like compounding, so that your savings and time can work for you, but I am here to tell you mastering the technicalities of investing is not necessary. In fact, simple wins every time as we will discuss later.

Even if you get caught up in the excitement of that world, to invest, you first must save. Saving is an emotional and behavioral process. It is a far more challenging hurdle than investing.

Together, we are going to take back personal finance and make it synonymous with saving. Not debt. Not investing. Saving matters most of all. And the timing of the advice is everything. Get it before it's too late, before you make the mistakes most of us have made and many will not come back from.

Consider the advice that I have heard over and over. It comes from a woman in her 50s who has nothing to her name. At some point in our meeting, it dawns on her that she will have to make extreme changes to get on track for retirement. Often, her eyes well with tears, and sometimes tears fall. Then, she tells me that if she could just go back to her former self, she would do one thing differently: save.

Let's rewrite the story of our college graduate and make her our heroine.

THE INSPIRATION:
PAY YOURSELF FIRST AND SAVE 10

"I want to *want* to make money. I don't want to *need* to make money."
— Farnoosh Torabi[7]

Olivia is setting out on a new path. On the old path, Olivia made the common mistake of funneling her money through her operating expenses, or daily lifestyle, first. The idea was that what was leftover each month could be used to pay off debt or to save. Unfortunately, one-off expenses keep gobbling up anything left over each month. Student loan monthly payments will start coming due in six months, but there is nothing left to pay them. She is heading for the nightmare scenario of student loans *and* credit cards.

Let's turn this upside down. Instead of funneling money through spending, hoping some ends up coming out the bottom to pay down student loan debt and save, how about we funnel money through saving and debt repayment and *then* allocate the rest for spending? In fact, let's funnel our money through different forms of saving, starting with retirement and paying off the student loan debt aggressively (as a form of saving), then starting an emergency fund account. From there, we will start saving ahead for future vacations, car repairs, and gifts. Then, what's left over will be available for spending.

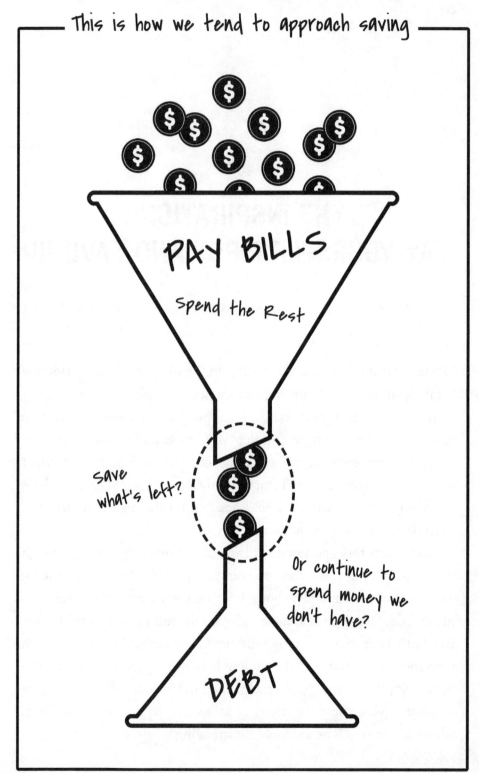

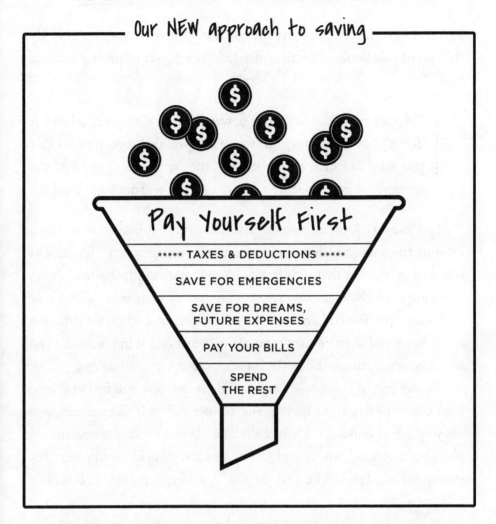

Our NEW approach to saving

Pay Yourself First

***** TAXES & DEDUCTIONS *****

SAVE FOR EMERGENCIES

SAVE FOR DREAMS,
FUTURE EXPENSES

PAY YOUR BILLS

SPEND
THE REST

By working together to change the story, we will make Olivia not just a heroine, but the boss of her own life. Building up retirement and cash reserves, easily paying off student loan debt, and avoiding credit card debt achieves this, and through Olivia's story, you will establish your own story, even if your starting point in life looks different. Maybe you don't have student loan debt (or you have far more debt). Maybe you will not live at home. The same principles will apply to dramatically differing circumstances. The very basics of making you the master of your own financial destiny involve learning how to use a system that, once in place, will be adjustable throughout your life, at any fluctuation in income, with any changing life goals or retirement aspirations. By the end of this book, you will understand the power of paying yourself first.

> "Money equals opportunity, power, control, autonomy. Maybe it doesn't buy happiness, but it does buy you the opportunities that you want to feel like your best self, the experiences you want, the agency you need to leave a bad situation." — Farnoosh Torabi[8]

Join me on a journey into the psychology of our brains, an insider's view of the industry that your money will engage with, the current status of women in that industry as consumers and professionals, and, most importantly, *how* you can take control of your money in a way that brings joy. We will arrive at the conclusion that when we cut out a lot of noise and a lot of alienation, there is just one thing women need to worry about, think about, dream about, and focus on: saving.

By the end of this book, I am confident that you will feel saving to your core—to live it, to love it, and to internalize it. Remember, you are young and making a lifetime decision. If you create a foundational philosophy around money and saving, you are more likely to adopt this system for life. It won't be a whim or a New Year's resolution. It will be a life practice.

If I was just telling you to save and how to save for retirement, this book would be short. It would join the piles of books telling you to save and how easy it is, only for you to put it down and still not save. It would just be a financial diet that you go on until you see a certain number, only to see those spending numbers rise up again with a vengeance after a much-needed treat-yourself day.

Instead of stopping there, once we establish saving for retirement and paying down debt, we will move to a cash management system that will work for your entire life. It will make you the boss, or the Chief Financial Officer (CFO), of your personal budget. I promise to never use

Budget

A word that has terrified children of the Depression-era generation and the generations that followed.

Synonyms: deprivation, misery, loneliness, friendlessness.

the word budget again. We will instead say "cash flow management," because the point of money is to bring the optimal amount of joy and security for each individual who has it.

I did not invent the cash flow management system that I'm going to share with you. It is a system I learned personally from a nationally renowned financial planner, Marty Kurtz. He would not say that he fundamentally invented a pay yourself first system either. This is an age-old concept that he adapted for a modern era of banking and credit card technology. Essentially, age-old wisdom works to help you find the optimal use of each dollar, but age-old systems of cash and checkbooks don't. He created an actual planning tool, called the First Step Cash Management System™, that could be used by a financial advisor in a planning relationship with a client to set up a pay yourself first system. I personally have a subscription to this tool and have used it in client relationships. It is an ingenious integration into a client relationship that clients are asking for from their advisors. Budgeting used to be thought of as the thing that only those with lower incomes wanted to do, but financial advisors are starting to realize that people of all income levels want to have better control of their cash flows.

The basic idea is to automate savings for large ticket items first and then spend the rest.

The likelihood of you having an advisor is nil, but as we discuss later, you will do just fine. You can apply basic and important principles of automation and saving first on your own, and I have adapted the pay yourself first cash flow system for young people getting started in life who won't have someone looking over their shoulder.

The point of this book is to inspire and explain how you can apply this to your life.

Book Roadmap

1. **You'll drool over a compound interest chart.** (This is totally about to happen.)

2. **You'll learn why automation can be better than inspiration.**

3. **You'll learn why I'm interested in being one of the first people to talk to you about money: so you won't be like so many women left behind in the financial world.**

4. **You'll understand why the financial advice industry is not currently built to advise you in your stage of life, but that's okay.**

5. **You'll learn the cash flow system in steps:**

   Step 1: Pay Yourself First/Save into Your Retirement Fund. (You could stop here, but Steps 2, 3, and 4 will take your money and your life to the next level.)

   Step 2: Pay for Future Expenses. (Understand that rather than relying on a backward-looking system that attempts to control your spending through personal shame, you are committing to a forward-looking system that helps you take pride in taking care of yourself as you prepare for inevitable future expenses. This is how previous generations budgeted before Americans became consumed by debt culture.)

   Step 3: Pay Your Bills.

   Step 4: Spend the Rest. (Can I get a Wah! Wah! This is REAL, y'all.)

6. **You'll read some wrap-up info, learn how Olivia applies this system as her life unfolds, and consider an invitation to for-**

mally join the **Save10 movement** so that you can receive the support of many other women making the same decision(s) you are.

7. **You'll read the last page and close the book. You will understand the power of paying yourself first and saving 10% for retirement. You will understand how to implement the 4 Steps.**

8. **You will be prepared to ladysplain money to others and bring other women to experience the joy of saving and managing their own money.**

Let's get started!

This is Not About Investing

What frustrates me most about the financial industry for the average person is that there are piles of information on highly technical approaches like investing, which mask the simplest but most profound advice.

A young woman once came into my office to discuss her 401(k) that I managed. Her dad was concerned about the investing options and whether they had a chance of beating the market. A few questions in, I found out she was saving just 2% of her income, had over $8,000 in credit card debt, and had a $600/month car payment.

As our discussion unfolded, and she realized I wasn't going to run out the door in shock and horror at her situation, the conversation changed. The constant dinner table conversations on investments made her feel the need to come in to talk about investments. But what she really needed to do was slay the debt and increase her savings, perhaps then getting around to debating the relative merits of her investment choices.

This obsession with investments distracts from the more obvious actions people need to take to build their wealth. For instance, there are people who have chronically undersaved their whole lives and walk in telling me that they "don't want to lose any money. No risk." But let's think about the spending they engaged in throughout their lives. Spending money is a guaranteed rate of negative return. To zero. You had money. You gave it to someone else. Now you don't have that money.

So why would we ever obsess about investments when the elephant in the room is eating your money, peanut by peanut, in rent, car payments, and dining out? Because that's what we think we're supposed to do. What I'm telling you now is that instead of worrying about growing (or losing) your money in investments, I can give you a way to take back some of those peanuts and thus worry less about investing being some kind of silver bullet.

This is about to get really fun. **Here is your official permission: Do not do what you think you are supposed to do. Instead of worrying about investing first, spend your time and efforts on saving first.**

More precisely, I want you to save 10% of everything you make. Actually, let's say it a better way: I want you to pay yourself first with 10%.

In her book *Mindful Money*, my mentor, Linda Bessette, says, "Always save. Save consistently. Save no matter what."[9] You probably have more of a chance to save than any other living generation. The ones before us were still living in the wake of pensions, where people worked for a company all their lives and were then taken care of by that company in their retirement through monthly payments. The problem is pensions went away and went away too quietly. People were lulled by this feeling or understanding that it all just kind of works out. Pull up newspaper articles about the retirement crisis on a given day, and you now know that's not the case. You are the first generation starting out a life in the wake of the tragedy of a lot of people who can't retire on their own terms. There is no more false sense of security.

"From the perspective of choice architecture, defined-benefit plans have one large virtue: they are forgiving to even the most mindless of Humans."   — Thaler and Sunstein[10]

For natural savers, the choice to save feels right because saving is its own reward. But what about the rest of you who—like I used to—think that while saving seems like the *right* thing to do, can't escape the notion that going without makes life feel somehow devoid of joy?

People with those feelings and expressing variations on this theme sit in front of me on a daily basis, often repeating the words that make saving sound like a death wish: "I believe in enjoying life today."

If you find yourself saying these or similar words, you've fallen into a common trap. It may sound true, but on closer examination, it is not true. What we want to save is a minimum of 10%. That is a small amount of money. Many would argue it should be higher. So, you *are* enjoying your money today. Ninety whole percent of it. Well, you and the government are enjoying it. (We will talk about taxes later.) In an interview at Google, financial guru Paula Pant makes the point that there is still inherent enjoyment that can come from watching your money accumulate. The argument she made to this young, ambitious crowd went as follows: "When you tell someone in their 20s to delay gratification, that sounds awful. I'm not delaying gratification. I am super-gratified by watching my net worth grow. I'm super-gratified by looking at the numbers in this account and watching them get bigger."[11]

But to these points on living in the now and reducing current joy for future joy, I have lived them all. The arguments I have to save a large percentage of my income now would be difficult arguments for my former life. Everyone has a different savings journey. In my own life, saving begot saving. It wasn't until I saved a little that I thought saving a little more could be even better. Tasting the freedom and excitement and possibility of it got me off the sidelines. It wasn't until I saw that saving a lot meant that in my 30s, I got to let go of my 6:30 am to 5 pm job to pursue my dream of starting a company. In his 40s, my husband got to walk away from a 7 am to 5 pm job to start a company where working one night a week nearly replaced the salary of working those days.

For me, it took seeing that in action to realize something profound: Saving is ultimate power. It's the ability to walk away from a day job to a business where you are the boss and don't feel like work is work anymore. It's the ability to negotiate a better business deal. It's the ability to get a better interest rate on a home loan. It's the power to live life on your own terms and no one else's.

As I mentioned before, I've heard every money story, good and bad. What I have never heard is anyone express regret about saving. No one ever says, "I wish I hadn't saved so much." I guess there can be extreme cases of miserly behavior, but young people who talk to me about growing up in those households almost uniformly express admiration for their parents' frugality.

B.C. Krygowski, a physician who is a thought leader in the financial independence movement, describes the difference well. "A miser is a person who lives in wretched circumstances so they can hoard money. Being frugal means being economical and choosing cheaper, but acceptable ways to have the same type of lifestyle that still brings me joy daily."[12] When parents have a lot of credit card debt for the sake of letting kids experience seeing the world through travel or letting them try new activities, often that's actually not what the kids want. They would forgo any trip or activity to avoid overhearing the fights at night about the credit card bill that just arrived or the general anxiety and tension that looms in any debtor household. If you are reading this, and that's what your home life felt like, you know what I mean. And I will ask you, is there anything your parents could have bought you that you would have valued more than peace in your home life?

Compound Interest Chart

Soon, a chart is going to flash in front of you. There is a chance that the mere glimpse of this chart will be enough for you to sell everything and open a retirement account. Ok, here goes ... 1, 2, and ...

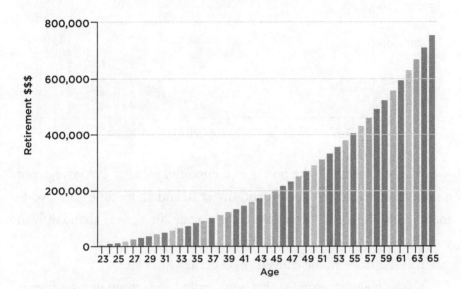

We will use Olivia for this example. She is 23, makes $45,000 per year and saves 10%, or $4,500 per year into a retirement account. Just to keep this simple, assume Olivia gets no raises, her investments grow modestly at 5.6% annually, net of fees, and she receives no company match. By age 65 she ends up with just over $750,000, even though all she deposited over those years was a little over $190,000.

Now, let's assume she didn't get the benefit of the advice to save 10% from the beginning. Instead, she started saving 10% 15 years later in her 30s. Here is what her retirement would look like: a hair under $290,000. So in a span of 42 years, shaving those first 15 years takes a lot more off than one would think.

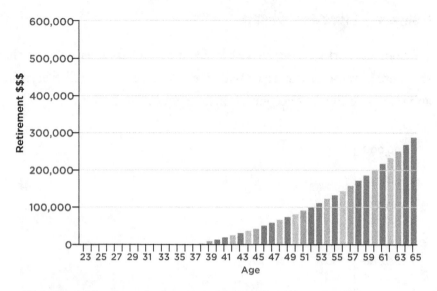

That, my friend, is the power of compound interest. Every year, put a little money into an account and invest it, and allow time and investments to work in your favor. If you are in your 20s, time is abundantly in your favor, so you can use this to your advantage.

This might be it, the conversion experience.

Maybe you just dropped this book, called your mom or your friend, and told them you are IN. You will from this day forward save 10% of everything you ever make and invest as we talk about later. Awesome! Even if this chart was enough to convince you, I hope you will read on.

If you didn't just have the conversion experience, don't be dismayed. There is something for everyone in this book. I promise you will be saving 10% by the end.

THE PERSPIRATION

"The biggest determinant of your success depends on your ability to get out of your own way." —Jimmy Turner[13]

For some, inspiration is the path to saving money. For others, there is automation.

You might be like I was and completely convinced that savings would be a great thing to have, starting . . . next month. The inner dialogue goes something like, *This month it's tough to put more in because I've got the big October wedding that will be the budget buster. Oh, it's November—talk about the worst month to save as I stare down Christmas. December—of course not. January—gotta pay off that credit card from the holiday.* And so on, and so on, and so on. Next month will *always* be the month to get that savings account open and put in the $100 minimum deposit.

When I give this example in group presentations, people in the room are nodding so hard I worry about a neck sprain. It's a rite of adult passage to open a savings account and maybe successfully fund it once, only to pull it out right away.

To be clear, if you opened a savings account as a kid, put regular deposits into it and didn't spend it, and now you have $15,000 saved, congratulations. That's amazing, and you will find the directions in the book pretty easy to implement. Just swing by the bank, withdraw a few hundred in ones temporarily, and use those ones to pat yourself on the back for a few minutes. Then re-deposit them.

Ok, back to my spenders, which is most of you and also me. All you have to do is agree with me in theory that saving is a smart idea. Then, sprint to the closest 401(k) store and buy one of those.

401(k)

The world's lamest name to describe the world's most important way for people to save for retirement. Other versions of a 401(k) for nonprofit and government employers are 403(b)s and 457(b)s, respectively.

401(k) retirement plans are AWESOME. They don't actually get sold in stores, but bear with me for a second. Imagine your retirement plan encrusted in bling, if you like, or with rainbows, unicorns, and stars arched over it. Whatever look suits your fancy, they are built and designed for us, the spenders. Here's why: We get to make one decision at one point in time to save. Then we get out of the way. It's one choice, but it's big. If we are already working and making a paycheck, the decision can be a little hard. Our paycheck gets lowered in order to send money away into that beautiful retirement account. If we are not working yet, it's easy—because we didn't even know what our paycheck was going to look like anyway.

Once we say "yes," the 401(k) plan does all the work.

I hate vacuuming more than any household chore, and a Roomba® would be life-altering. Imagine never having to look at the dirty rug, guilt growing as the filth continues to accumulate, only to get to a breaking point, then finally heading to the closet that has the vacuum in it. Only, it's been a while, so fishing it out means a pile of coats and dirty laundry have to come tumbling out of the closet first. After finally getting it out, you have to find an outlet not already used and one close enough to not run out of cord. Then, to be thorough, you've got to move the coffee table and chairs. Terrible. Vacuuming is the worst chore ever.

Enter the Roomba. It sits there, stealthily hidden from plain sight. When you leave the house, it undocks and quietly does its business (which was formerly your business) throughout the day. It will be sweetly docked away by the time you come home, lest you see it and conjure memories of just how bad it was when you had to vacuum.

The 401(k) is just as fantastic as the Roomba. Roombas are expensive, though. So is the 401(k). Only the expense is you saving—for yourself. It has an upfront cost (your first savings deposit) which will make you feel significant pain as that paycheck goes down. But, buy one of those 401(k)s, and it sits completely out of sight. When your paycheck hits, it gathers up your savings. You never have to see it. And your lifestyle adapts so that you don't feel the second, third, or fourth savings deposits like the first.

But there's a way to get the 401(k) for "free," meaning you will save and not feel the requisite pain of saving. Yep, your 401(k) can feel free IF you get those savings taken out on day one. If this is your first job, and you don't have a paycheck yet, there is no pain. You didn't know what your paycheck was really going to look like in the first place, and you just build your lifestyle around whatever your take-home pay is.

If you have been working, you will feel the pain this one time as the auto deposit of your paycheck is less than it was the previous month. By the next paycheck, you don't even feel the pain of saving because we humans are adaptable creatures. It's like taxes . . . Do you actually know what you paid in taxes on your last paycheck? Probably not. Do you know your actual health insurance premium? Possibly not (especially if your parents still pay it—ahem). How about your monthly parking fee that comes out of the paycheck? Doubtful! Many of us just don't think about those things that come out of our check. They disappear before we consider them.

Why don't we do this for ourselves? For our futures? Right? Time after time, I meet and consult with all these wonderful people who have lived great lives, raised great kids, worked really hard, and are getting into their 60s with nothing to show for their whole working lives. Nothing. They can't ever stop working, lest they retire into poverty. They can't stop working even if they have a major injury or illness. They paid everyone else, from car dealers to health insurance companies to colleges, but they never paid anything to themselves. They are stuck.

You do not have to be one of these wonderful, stuck people. Imagine if you can choose right now to pay yourself first, and you don't even know the difference. The money was never there in the first place. You are never reminded of the past you who was not a saver, who couldn't save, who started the savings account only to stop funding it and pillage it by the next month.

You won't pillage this account because you will feel like it was never there. It gets locked in a vault, out of sight and out of mind. And automation is the miracle. You could even theoretically live the most irresponsible life, the most thoughtless, carefree, roller coaster life, but there is that 401(k) quietly cleaning up after you. Your 401(k)roomba.

Automation is the key. The 401(k) is the hottest fashion right now. Everyone is—or should be—doing it. But wait, there's more than the 401(k). I'm also going to teach you how to automate other savings accounts so that you can kick back and relax with the knowledge that you've put everything in motion for yourself.

We'll talk about how you get one of those 401(k)s later.

WOMEN WILL LEAD US OUT OF THIS SAVINGS CRISIS

Yes, I am looking at you. I recently had a retirement plan encounter that still has me smiling. An older woman with median income walked into the room to enroll in our new retirement plan. We chatted, and she said she kind of hoped to be able to retire in the next couple of years. "Would it be possible?" she asked. I inquired how much she had saved so far. She looked down when she said she didn't know. What percentage are you saving? Again, she didn't know. I told her no problem and went to look it up. When I saw the line on the computer screen with her account balance and a 15% savings rate underneath, it took my breath away. I walked back into the room with a grin and asked her when she had chosen to contribute 15%. She said as long as she had worked there (a long time). I revealed the amount she had in her account, and she just smiled and chuckled in disbelief. She asked if it was enough to retire. Indeed, it was enough for more than one retirement. When I asked what made her choose that savings rate, she didn't know. Perhaps it was intentional at the time, and she had since forgotten. Perhaps it was arbitrary. The motivation doesn't matter. It's the action that does.

Ladies, this is the story you want to have. One where you make a single decision at one point in your life, then automate it, and one day wake up to find that the money you need is there. This woman never stressed over saving. It happened automatically, just like her taxes and her medical insurance premiums, only over the course of her whole life, she was also paying herself first. Keep reading, and I'll show you how to make her story your story, to be prepared not only to retire when you want, but to build a pile of cash that will be a freeing companion on your journey to build a happy life.

But first, let's look at why I am so interested in speaking to young women.

There is no way to describe the feeling of sitting on a retirement account and a pile of cash in the bank that you put there. Women who have it describe it as a sense of power, or deep security, but most often as freedom. I have seen women walk away from toxic jobs and relationships because they had a pile of cash. You don't need a job waiting in the wings to leave another job when you have a pile of cash. Sometimes you have to scrub "stuff" out of your psyche, take a break, ponder what you really want to do, or figure out who you really want to work for. (Maybe yourself?) The only way to do that is with a pile of cash.

I have certainly had lots of women list all the reasons why that cash pile wasn't high on the priority list, from living in the now to making sure that their kids have everything they need. But what they've shared is that they had never experienced the security of sitting on a pile of cash that they put there. Because that pile is hard to build and can take several years, it is much easier to dismiss its importance than face the ramifications of what happens when you don't save.

Build Your Cash Pile Now: Not Piling = Not an Option

Sometimes people list saving for retirement or saving into an emergency fund as if these are menu items. "I'll take one mortgage, two car payments, and, sure, throw in 3% savings for retirement." We still treat saving as an option—as something we do with the leftovers (if there are any) after we're done spending.

But we are robbing our future selves and our freedom by treating it as an arbitrary amount that we can throw in or not. Think about paying your federal income taxes. Is that a menu item for discussion? Do you get to decide how much to pay? How about health insurance?

I am asking you to build a pile of money, both in your retirement and savings accounts. Most will be invested, and the rest will stay in cash. In fact, as you will read, I would love for you to build several money piles. You may have a burning reason to build your pile right now, and that sure does make it easier. But even if you don't have the fire in the belly for it now, I want you to trust me. Your reasons and imagination for having a money pile might grow alongside that money pile. Don't deprive your future self of that level of freedom and opportunity.

Later, we will walk through why you can't look for direction from the financial industry in its current state to help us build those piles of money. Many women are disconnected from their money because they feel disconnected from the financial industry. We have to make the industry more friendly toward women, but in the meantime, it cannot be a source of financial avoidance in your life.

What I have personally witnessed is that women do one of three things: they muscle their own way through financial decisions by reading blogs and books and listening to podcasts (rare), they ask their spouses or someone else they trust to do it (pretty common), or they delay it (most common). The latter is why I see a parade of 50-year-old women year after year through our retirement plans who have nothing, nada, zilch saved. It's not that they disagree with saving or retiring, it's just that they haven't gotten around to it. And the reason they often haven't gotten around to it is that they didn't understand it, it never got brought up, or they didn't trust the person talking to them about it. The list goes on. And, here's the thing—they are all fair points. I was the girl in the back of the class who would never raise her hand. It wasn't that I lacked confidence. No, it was that I thought too much. By the time I arrived at an opinion or decision, the conversation had moved on. I didn't want to speak unless I was an expert on something or felt I had greater knowledge on it than the rest of the class, so the opportunity passed me by every time.

You might be nodding in agreement with me, but, my friend, we have to act differently when it comes to our money. We have to act in an environment of risk and imperfect information.

The ones who leave it to spouses often get a worse deal. It turns out spouses aren't saving enough either, certainly not for two retirement accounts. So many women leave money to their partner when they go into marriage, assuming that wealth will come from that union. Indeed, the promise is there. Merging two households and those efficiencies is an incredible opportunity to build wealth. Instead, we see the opposite happening. We see savings rates too low for both people living in that household.

In 2019, the U.S. had more single women in their 50s than in history, including both divorced women and those who never married. I ask you, which women were financially better off? The never marrieds. A recent study from the Center for Retirement Research confirmed that 46% of married women versus 39% of single women were at risk for not being able to maintain their working-years lifestyle once they reached retirement. This is because of a stronger savings rate alongside better social security. Married women who didn't work or worked less because of caregiving ended up filing for half of their ex-husband's social security, which is on average less than a single working woman's social security payment.[14]

Please, I beg you. As Linda Bessette so eloquently states in conversation, "The opposite of retirement is work," and you do not want to sentence yourself to a best-case scenario that most likely means you'll be working for the rest of your life. You want options.

If you get your finances in order and keep them that way, saving and investing through your working career, then not only will you change the course of your life, you are going to change others' lives. Women don't operate in a vacuum—we operate in a peer-to-peer world. And never have there been more forums for women to gather and talk about money. (I've co-created one private Facebook group called Save10, which you can join. Our community of saving-oriented women will welcome you and your questions, challenges, and anecdotes with open arms.)

Remember the story of the unwitting saver? What if her story was ours? We work hard our whole lives and wake up one day ready to stop working, spoil the grandkids, travel, and have control of our own days, so we go fetch the login for our accounts and delightedly open them up to see that, yes, we are able to make the move we're hungry for. Monday, we can walk into work, give our notice, and walk away triumphantly with the ability to continue living in the same house, driving the same car, eating the same food, and drinking the same wine—all enjoyed with the cherry on top of more time to ourselves.

But that is not our story just yet.

Women are being disproportionately affected by the retirement crisis. We live longer, we make less money, and our careers are disrupted more frequently through caregiving, whether to our children or our parents. We are disproportionately affected by divorce.

And the world is dying to tell you that it's because women are irrational and bad with money. We buy expensive shoes and can't stop our latte addictions. Nothing burns me up more than this argument! But the statistics are what they are. We will go through them. You can see what the rest of the world sees—that women continue to lag behind men in money. BUT—thank goodness for this amazing BUT—if you look deeper at the studies, if you look at the financial industry from 15,000 feet, then you'll understand that there is a story being completely missed.

This is not about you catching up. No, no, no. This is about you stepping up and leading. There is a gender leadership void in the financial industry. Of the 87,270 people who hold the CFP® designation, only 23% of them are women.[15] A 2016 *Harvard Business Review* study estimated that only 20% of board seats of financial institutions are held by women.[16] At the top, it is more obvious with only 12% of leaders of financial services firms being women. The study showed that while open gender discrimination seemed to be stamped out, unfortunately, "unconscious biases and gender-role expectations that disadvantage women have not."

The industry is lacking women in leadership and in advisory roles, and at the same time the industry is not providing widespread benefit to our personal finances. A future where so many people retire into poverty is not a future any of us want to live in, whether or not we are the ones in poverty. I hope you will gain a deeper understanding of money and take control of your finances. My greater hope is that some of you reading this will not only want to consume the information, but share it.

Know Better, Do Better

While women objectively should be saving aggressively, far more aggressively than our male counterparts to make up for a longer life span, gaps in employment, caregiving, etc., the opposite is what we are actually doing. We are undersaving, from boomers to millennials. What's the reason? I can tell you firsthand—avoidance. We don't do that which we don't understand.

When I started a new job fresh out of grad school, after sitting for my badge photo and choosing my health insurance, among a dozen other decisions, I was asked a question that was presented as being of equal importance to which deck I wanted to park my car in. "What percentage would you like to defer into the 401(k) plan?" The huh? Granted, I knew what a 401(k) plan was, and I knew I needed to save, of course, but how much should I save? "And look at this list of investments." A little overwhelmed, I remember looking at the HR rep and asking her what most people chose. She said 5% and then suggested I could pick the investments myself. I remember writing down the 5% and then hastily picking the investments, promising myself that I would come back and change everything when I had a chance to think about it. Only I never did. I never changed anything. Because I never thought about it again. Tell me—when would it have come up in casual conversation with the girlfriends? "Oh my gosh, have you seen the latest fund line-up in our 401(k) plan? That mid-cap value fund is HOT!" "Oohhhhh yes, but I personally have my eye on that emerging markets fund. How exotic." Or, "I have been deliberating this pro/con list for weeks to get the right percentage into my 401(k). Can I run it by you?"

Yeah, none of that. It never came up. It *doesn't ever* come up. We do not have casual, or formal, or ANY conversations about money. Shoot, even if we did, in perfect situations, tell me the day it would have seemed like a good idea to go to HR to lower my paycheck in order to increase my savings for retirement. The day doesn't come because once the box is checked, there are loads of reasons not to go back. You don't have to be actively in disagreement with savings to have the same outcome as someone who merely doesn't think about saving. In both situations, you end up broke.

As mentioned before, the reason women are lagging behind in savings is not lattes and shoes. Society makes it sound like we are consciously making choices to spend versus save, and on a daily basis we are actively choosing to spend at the detriment of saving. But you know that is not the case. I know that is not the case. I can tell you that generations before you are not saving because we don't understand how to do it, how much we need to do it, or when we need to do it. And when we don't understand, a lot of us just freeze. We choose not to act. In the absence of perfect information, we don't do anything. Thaler and Sunstein assume in their book, *Nudge*, that "most of these workers are just spacing out or procrastinating rather than making a reasoned decision that they have a better use for their money."[17] Let's not space out or procrastinate.

Case in point: one study shows that this gender savings gap may be closing thanks to a program called auto enroll. This is a concept born out of a body of research in economics that proves the premise of economics—the rational consumer—is wrong. Think about how your brain is constructed. The majority of your brain mass is dedicated to animalistic instincts, and those are mainly to protect you from acute dangers. They are not there to help you wrestle with subtle, long-term decisions. Saving, unfortunately, is one of those subtle, long-term decisions, so our animalistic brain acts irrationally when it comes to saving decisions. It prefers us to spend on acute needs. Shoes! Lattes! Just kidding.

Enter the field of libertarian paternalism—yep, ladies, prepare to get mansplained cuz there still ain't a lotta ladies in econ. It's essentially a way to maintain freedom of choice but manipulate those choices to help people make better ones.

One such example of libertarian paternalism is auto enroll. Companies can set this up as a default option into their retirement plans. Instead of having participants make a choice to join the plan, they are automatically put into the plan. If the company you work for has auto enroll, the default, do-nothing option is enrollment and the action becomes choosing *not* to join the plan. It turns out this "small change" is remarkably effective since most people don't take the action. The conversation no longer puts the onus and decision on the employee regarding how much to save and where to invest. Instead, the company says to the employee, "Unless you choose otherwise, we are going to automatically put you at X% savings rate, invested in Y investment." In other words, when we start work, unless we proactively change it, the company automatically helps us to save money (and save ourselves from ourselves and our irrational animal brains in the process).

It works. Since companies have been making this change, for the first time, we have a generation of retirement savers (go Gen Z-ers!) closing the gender savings gap. Women are saving a lot more than they were before AND catching up to male counterparts.[18] So now that we've pulled back the curtain, let's stop talking about lattes and shoes.

While auto enroll won't take us over the finish line since it is usually set up at 3% to 6% (still undersaving), it is working for women to close the savings gap with men. The reason it works? Well, let's go back to the moment we have to make the retirement plan decision during enrollment at our company. We look at it and hear all the jargon and feel just as overwhelmed. Only this time, instead of declining until we have the time to learn more (which studies show we are not likely to revisit), we allow ourselves to be defaulted into the plan saving at the default savings rate. In other words, we are still kicking the can down the road of understanding the retirement plan and making the optimal personal saving and investing decision, but at least we are saving something in the meantime.

I am not advocating for you to let auto enroll define whether you retire one day. As I mentioned, most of the auto enrolls we see today are at 3% to 6%, when we really need to be saving 10%. Anything less, while it is something, is not enough to retire. Companies breathe a sigh of relief if you allow them to auto enroll you into the retirement plan at 6%. From their perspective, the current retirement crisis is severe. If half of 50-year-olds have nothing saved, and a 20-something comes along saving 6%, companies consider that a win. But you can do more.

Now that we can cross irrational consumerism off the societal list of "reasons women don't save," let's move on to how allegedly illiterate we are on money. Sure, at face value, on paper, we may appear that way. In a large-scale financial literacy study done across the U.S., Germany, and the Netherlands, both male and female participants were administered the "big three"—the most common and widely acceptable measures of financial literacy that cover simple interest rate calculations, how inflation works, and risk diversification. Consistent with results from other countries, men in the U.S. answered 38% of the questions correctly, compared to women answering 22%.[19]

In this study and a meta-analysis of financial literacy across 14 countries, the gender gap is large and undeniable, even taking into account marital status, education, income, and other socioeconomic characteristics. They even found a gender gap in financial literacy among the young—despite younger women having higher education levels and labor force participation than previous generations.

Embedded in the study is something more striking than the financial literacy score itself. It turns out that women, more than men, were disproportionately more likely to respond that they didn't know the answer rather than take a guess. At first blush, you might think that is weak or timid. But what if admitting that you don't know something when it comes to money is actually a major strength, especially better than thinking we know more than we do, or being confident in our ability to take good guesses?

In *Thinking in Bets,* world poker champion Annie Duke argues "What makes a decision great is not that it has a great outcome. A great decision is the result of a good process, and that process must include an attempt to accurately represent our own state of knowledge. That state of knowledge, in turn, is some variation of I'm not sure."[20]

Why is this important? Well, there are easy decisions in financial literacy that you know right now. Saving some percentage of your money is right. Staying out of credit card debt is a good idea. But most financial decisions are not so crystal clear, and we have to operate in a fair amount of uncertainty, particularly when it comes to investing. "I'm not sure" will come in handy at that time, as long as you see it as a place of power and not weakness—if that uncertainty does not have a paralyzing effect.

Annie Duke has linked the same benefits of acknowledging and embracing uncertainty around decisions of champion poker players to those who invest well. What makes a good poker player? "They embrace that uncertainty and, instead of focusing on being sure, they try to figure out how *unsure* they are, making their best guess at the chances that different outcomes will occur."[21] This is my prescription for you. Know and understand saving for retirement. Know and understand the best buckets for saving for retirement. Know and understand that saving ahead for large ticket items (both expected and unexpected) is far better than going into debt for them.

On the rest? Please, continue to not be sure, to not know. It will lead to better decisions on your money. We'll get to that in a second.

We need financial literacy in high school, especially so our young people can learn the obvious lessons on saving and avoiding crippling debt that we are sure of. If you didn't get it, however, do not be dismayed. It turns out that financial education is best given or obtained at the time you are *actually* making your financial decisions. For example, high school students are best served by financial education on saving, something they can more easily take action on in the moment. Of lesser benefit is theoretical education on investing in the stock market, something that is best learned while doing but inaccessible to most high school students. I assume that if you are reading this book right now, you are at the decision point on saving and investing. Or, this education is timed perfectly as both of those are available and actionable to you. You have not missed the boat.

In our company, we treat financial wellness and our retirement plans as the time and place for people to learn fundamental financial concepts, especially saving, and to take action on that education. In our experience, when armed with sound education and advice that comes at the right time, *they make great decisions.*

A woman in her late 20s approached me after a keynote I gave at a conference on saving 10% for retirement. A single mom, she struggled and ultimately succeeded to get out of credit card debt, but she had not begun to accumulate adequate savings. There, on the spot, she pulled out her cell phone, logged into her mobile retirement account app, and pulled up the screen to reveal her savings rate. It was 2%. And right there while I watched, she increased that number to 10%. I asked her if she was ready for the paycheck change. She looked me square in the eyes and said it didn't matter. She heard my argument for why saving 10% was how much she needed to save, so she was doing it.

A couple of weeks later, I checked back in with her and asked her how that first paycheck was with the new savings rate. She said it meant having to make some subtle lifestyle changes, but it was not hard. I asked her what made her do it on the spot without puzzling over it, and she said the decision-maker was seeing people she knew who wanted to but were not able to retire. Finding out the right percentage to save and where to put it was all she needed to get over the savings hurdle. In other words, the right education at the right time.

Don't Waste Brain Power Worrying About Investing (Even Though Women Are Pretty Good at It)

"You can't pick winning stocks. Don't feel bad. I can't either. Nor can the overwhelming majority of professionals in the business. The fact that this ability is so rare is the key reason why the very few who apparently can are so famous." — JL Collins[22]

Picking stocks to try to beat the stock market average return is still a pretty ubiquitous activity for people, from professionals to amateurs. Every news or financial channel seems to be sharing the latest stock picking tip to get you excited to go buy something "hot." The problem is that we aren't very good at it, professionals and amateurs alike. It has been described as a "loser's game," an argument echoed by Warren Buffet.[23] You would imagine that there would be some kind of comprehensive rating system to see how good and accurate professional stock pickers (aka analysts) are. Unfortunately, there really isn't a universal tracking system. We don't keep a database of all calls over time. We can't know if those purveyors of hot tips are making money for people

Stock Primer

A stock is a piece of ownership in a company. Think of your local dry cleaner; it is probably owned by an individual or a group of individuals. It's private, its finances are private, and its owners get to make all the decisions on how it is run. Some companies have the ability to grow big, but to do so requires a lot of money, more than they could borrow or obtain with private investors. So, they become public and open their financials for the world to see. They allow people like you and me to buy a piece of them, and those pieces—called shares, stocks, or equities—are traded on public exchanges. All day long, millions of shares trade hands as people take ownership of companies as a way to grow their money faster than savings accounts can grow their money with interest.

over time or losing them money (via the opportunity cost of being in the aggregate stock market).

Even though I believe picking stocks is not a great idea for most folks, I find it curious that in one study women outperform men at the task. In a study done by the *Journal of Accounting Research*, when researchers looked at the outcome of 2 million stock calls placed by 17,240 analysts covering 13,636 stocks, they found that, on average, women had a better performance for outcomes of those stock calls.[24] The idea was that women who self-selected into the job of analyst were more talented at what they were doing. The rest of them who didn't feel they were as good at it self-selected out of it.

Those are the professional stock pickers in the industry, but what about everyday people investing money for themselves? How do women compare to men?

A large study at the University of California at Berkeley tested the theory that overconfidence and excessive trading could lead to lower returns and that men tended to engage in those behaviors more than women. It compared the performance by gender from 1991–1997 in over 35,000 households. Indeed, the excessive trading impacted men's portfolios by nearly a full percentage point compared to women. According to the study, "Greater overconfidence leads to greater trading and to lower utility."[25]

The stock market is full of the companies which comprise it and the people who buy those stocks. And there are these real-time indicators of how stocks are performing at any given nano-second. They are called indices, and they will track various segments of the market. You might have heard of the Dow Jones or the S&P 500 or the Nasdaq. Each of those is called an index. Take the S&P 500 index. It tracks the performance of 500 stocks in the market, mostly the largest ones, which actually makes up about 80% of the market—therefore it's a very good proxy for how the whole market is doing.

The way most people buy stocks in the market is through mutual funds. The majority of mutual funds are considered to be "actively managed," meaning that a human being collects savings from investors, like you and me, and then buys and sells stocks and/or bonds (we'll get there later) on our behalf. Our hope is that this person will grow our money over time. In fact, we hope they will grow our money faster than the market average. Those fund managers promise to. And we keep believing them. These fund managers decide which stocks to put in their funds as a result of their own research regarding what those companies might do relative to other companies.

> **Mutual Fund**
>
> A fund that collects people's money and then buys stocks, bonds, or both for them.

How do these guys perform? If you guessed average, that makes sense. The S&P Dow Jones Indices has a research arm, called the SPIVA Scorecard. It tracks the actual performance of these actively managed mutual funds compared to the S&P 500 index. Do you want to guess what the running average of those actively managed funds is over time? As of mid-2019, "some 91.81% of active large-cap core stock fund managers over the past 15 years had underperformed the index they were trying to beat."[26]

What is the reason these money managers are underperforming every year? Collectively, they can't beat the fees they are charging in those funds. They get paid so much money. Their staff gets paid so much money. Their offices in New York are so fancy and expensive. When you add it all up, even if they make some lucky calls every now and then, it is just not enough to overcome how much it costs to operate.

I hope you are reading this and saying, "Wow, this is not at all what I expected. I thought I was missing something." All of that jargon, all of that complication is really not all that helpful to your needs. As it turns out, NONE of that matters. If you want to play the game and try to beat the market, read everything you can get your hands on, and find the best in the business, you still have less than a 10% chance of beating the market. Or, put another way, you have a greater than 90% chance of *underperforming* the market. Or put another way, the *more* effort you or someone you hire puts into your investments, the *worse* off your money will likely be.

In 2011, I first learned about something that would inspire me to create a new financial practice. With the radical simplification of investing, I could have a business running a financial plan only, focused largely on saving, without the need for us to physically invest money for clients. In other words, for the first time, I saw a vision where the advice industry could progress forward merely because investing went from something only the experts could do to something that artists, accountants, and doctors could all do, on their own, from a laptop or iPad.

What was this invention? It was called an index mutual fund. Instead of trying to beat the market, just join it. Buy the whole market. Don't try to pick winners. Don't hire people to try to pick winners. It is the opposite of active. You don't really care or need to beat your neighbor's stock performance. If the whole market is up 5%, you're cool with being up 5%. In 2019, the S&P 500 was up 30.43%. You would be cool being up just that much.

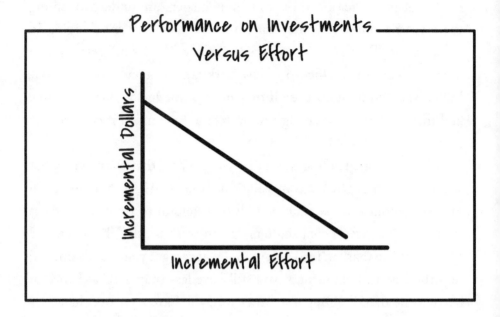

That objective to win, to beat the market, albeit patently flawed, has lit fires in professionals in the field since the dawn of the market. It's the Wall Street bull, chest beating, titan-of-industry goal to be a superior investor—to make your money grow faster than your neighbor's.

Dear financial industry, if we are going to enter into a relationship with you, we want a partnership and for what you offer to complement what we can offer. We will offer you our hard-earned savings, but we can tell you that what we don't want are attempts to beat the market. It's unpredictable. It makes promises it can't keep. Sure, it may seem glamorous for a couple years with spikes in the portfolio from good calls, you know, the doors opening for us, the roses that appear on no special occasion, the last-minute dash over to Europe. But lemme tell you, what most women want is steady and sturdy performance. We want you to make Tuesday and Thursday night dinner.

We want you at the parent teacher conferences. We want you to call shotgun on the next poopy diaper. When we open up our statements we want to see that you did just what the market did—not better. Not worse. Average.

One more interesting point. In recent studies of the relative performance of men and women investing, guess who tends to win? Women.[27] Go to my endnotes and annotated bibliography, and read up yourself. But the reason is precisely what is laid out above. For the most part, women are not inclined to actively invest. We usually buy for the long-term. We generally don't day trade. We adhere to the principals that are proven to make one perform average in the market. And I'm hoping that you're with me that in the world of investing, being average is #winning.

Let's return to the condition that women are unwittingly better stock pickers and investors but are largely missing from the industry as advisors and in leadership. We have generations of young girls who think money is interesting, but when they peek in the door of the finance class, they see it is mostly male. Perhaps when they talk to their college advisor about loving money, they are encouraged to become accountants and bookkeepers. It is no wonder that women are so lacking in professional finance careers.

Where this impacts you, whether you are an engineer or marketing professional, is that when you engage in the financial world, most commonly through your company retirement plan, it is not likely that your retirement plan advisor will be female. But as I hope I have proven, that is no cause for intimidation. You have every right to engage and ask questions, to save and to invest. In fact, we desperately need you at the table.

But First, Save

Now, let's get out of the macro financial industry and get down to you, young file clerk, doctor, lawyer, nurse, researcher, accountant, barista, sales manager, or dreamer and doer. You are just trying to figure out what to do, because you need to save. You need to invest. In study after study, women report feeling disconnected from the financial industry. They are less engaged, and less engagement means less likely to make a plan. They are less likely to hire a financial advisor or do their own plan, and without a plan are very unlikely to prepare for retirement. This is the problem. Back to our chart—again, we know that extra effort and investment of money and resources into outperforming investments ends up backfiring. But here is where extra effort can work: when it is almost entirely focused on saving (enough).

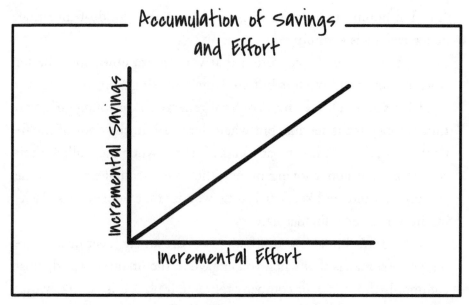

If we could reinvent the industry, THIS is what it would look like. All incremental effort would get spent and compensated for by helping people do one thing: save. All that complication and jargon built up by a focus on investing and trying to beat the market is a house of cards, meaning that if you focus on investing while undersaving, your finances will likely fall apart at some point. Thus, why this book is centered on the decision and practice of saving.

We've spent this first section identifying the disconnect between women and the financial industry. Now, let's see what women are asking for when it comes to finances. It might coincide with what you might want. A recent study by a research firm, Kantar, found that whereas men feel comfortable with investments as a proxy for money, "women feel a deep, emotional engagement" with their finances. To them money represents "both safety and success—or lack thereof." Some women even go on to see their care of money as a duty to family.[28]

Creating a plan to save and accumulate wealth is where we should start. A financial plan, not the narrow act of investing, represents the path to achieving our life dreams.

Closing Gender Disparities

Let's look at a fascinating experience in the state of Wisconsin. Officials there became aware of a gender gap in retirement contributions in the state and started a program called EMPOWER. The program used multi-media and peer-to-peer engagement to reach women and get them to save on the spot. They offered no incentives to participate, no time off, and they were probably convinced that few would show up. Incredibly, they reported that meeting after meeting was filled. One-on-one financial counseling sessions were booked up. The goal of EMPOWER was to create and reinforce the norm that talking about finances was accepted and encouraged. After the effort, female state employees' savings increased 2.6 percentage points, closing the gender gap by more than half.[29]

Dr. Jason Mizell, a surgeon and professor at the University of Arkansas for Medical Sciences (UAMS), decided that medical students didn't just need a one-hour lecture on investing—which is how many med schools handle financial education. Instead, he designed a semester-long elective personal finance course called the Business of Medicine with a weekly two-hour session on saving, budgeting, investing, paying down debt, medical coding, negotiation, and estate planning. What's the gender split for enrollment? Equal when you adjust for representation of gender in the entire med school class.

The answers to fixing the gender disparities in the industry are right here. And you are part of this change. You can benefit from it, and you can fuel it. We are seeing women talk about money for the first time through various social media and peer-to-peer structures. With passive investing, women are coming to see that they have an alternative to chasing investment returns not worth the money charged to do it. This is the perfect mix for change. This is the perfect time for you to take the plunge and get involved.

You don't have to do this alone.

As my friends will say, some with accompanying eyerolls, I can become fairly evangelical in my passion for getting people to save. But it comes from a place of authentic concern. Not many people have insight into the intense fear and anxiety felt by someone in her 60s who has lived a good life, worked hard, and raised kids, but is sentenced to one of two realities: work and work and work, despite physical ailments or weariness or, even worse, retire into poverty.

But as you know, at this moment it is still much easier to find people willing to give us debt to fuel a bigger lifestyle than to find someone who will help us save. Think about this. If you are on social media, can you post a picture of a new car or a picture of your savings contribution? The former will get you firecrackers and fist bump emojis. The latter—well, nothing—because you wouldn't share it in the first place, right?

We have to change this!

Save10 Could Save Us All

My unwavering desire to urge sweeping change in the way women think, talk about, and deal with their money is why I co-founded, with Stephanie Matthews, a movement called Save10. It's simple. We dream that you and 10,000 other women will commit to saving 10%. (At least 10,000 is our initial goal, but why stop there?)

Let's say you are working and not saving 10%. To sign up would mean a pay decrease. Decide to do it, and you'll wince at your first paycheck. By the second check you have probably forgotten. With every subsequent job change, you roll over your account balance and you robotically remember to select 10%. Cuz it's "what you do." Then you wake up as one of the rare people out there with the pleasure of living on your own terms, with the option to work or not to work. Wow. Imagine.

Remember the Wisconsin example? Its ultimate success was largely explained by the peer-to-peer support—Come join us! In partnership with the Women's Foundation of Arkansas, we launched a Save10 Facebook group, open to women everywhere, in July 2019. By October 2019 when we launched Save10 officially, 5,200 women had joined and are sharing money tips, celebrating debt repayments, and posting screenshots of the moment they increased their retirement savings rate to 10%.

Why women? It's not just because we are lagging behind men in savings and are disproportionately impoverished in retirement. The movement is aimed toward women because studies prove that teaching women to do anything has a compounding societal effect. That's why microfinance and disease eradication are aimed at women. We will spread the lessons and wealth.

Here is my call to you:

Take the Save10 challenge at save10challenge.com, get on the pay yourself first money system (explained just ahead), and tell all your friends. This is how I, you, we can fix this retirement crisis. Also, 10% of the royalty proceeds from this book go to the Women's Foundation of Arkansas to support Save10.

Not ready to click? I sincerely hope you will be by the end of this book. We need you.

THE FINANCIAL INDUSTRY

As an industry insider, I can tell you that your savings rate is the most important money decision you will ever make. My passion for the message of saving is deeper than a hunch or, as with many personal finance books, just from my own saving experience. Instead, my background in investments and subsequent experience starting a financial company informs my theory for why the message of saving is getting drowned out. The biggest issue I have with the industry is that it makes people feel like math experts are the only ones who can do well with their money. We conflate finance with math. How many marketing professionals or web designers say to me, "I am a creative, not a numbers person. I get lost in this stuff." Well, shoot, if you think the world of your money is profit and loss statement analysis, price-to-earnings ratios, and discounted cash flows, then, yeah, it probably does seem like a math degree is required to understand this stuff.

So, this is me climbing up a large ladder to the top of a building and shouting it from the rooftop: Artists, teachers, engineers, math and non-math people alike—join us! You are a money person! Money will help you pursue your dreams. Saving is for you! Don't believe me? Gosh, keep reading.

Growing up, like many young girls, I was convinced that I was not a math person, and no one could convince me otherwise. The story I told myself in my early years was that I was a great reader and super creative. I would certainly end up in a creative field.

The years only reinforced this narrative. But honestly, I was never at peace with it. I remember one day in the 7th grade, the math teacher announced that she would be selecting 5 students who would be moving into an accelerated math track. I remember thinking, "Oh by some miracle, pick me. PICK ME." Maybe I have an inner math prowess that only she sees, and she alone has realized that the way they teach math at this school just doesn't cater to my natural math genius. But no, no matter how they taught math at that school, I was not selected. The math ACT was a merciless exercise. I took it repeatedly, hoping that somehow dumb luck would help me answer those math problems better, but I never scored above a 23 on the math portion. The story continued unabated in college. "I am not good at math," I dramatically announced and chose remedial algebra, suffering through and barely emerging with my "B."

After college, I joined the Jesuit Volunteer Corps serving the homeless—a profession very light on math. A few years later, a little policy work I had done caught people's attention, and I found myself encouraged to apply to grad school at Harvard. Again, math reared its ugly head. I had to get a minimum math GRE score. And please understand, when I say minimum, I mean the minimum required to skid by into acceptance. I hired a math tutor, studied every available minute, and when I got the results, the score was literally the exact minimum acceptable. Putting the best spin on this, I guess you could say I nailed it, and that I hadn't studied a minute longer than was needed. Luckily, the rest of the application offset the poor math GRE showing, and I miraculously got in.

When I graduated with a master's in public policy, I moved home to Arkansas and got my "first real job" at an investment bank. My idea was essentially to be successful in business and allow myself the ability to volunteer and personally fund the public policy issues I wanted to take on. I also knew I would probably want to be involved in public service and that this career path would be a great launching point.

But the can I had been kicking down the road all those years ricocheted off the curb and hit me square between the eyes. For the first time in my life, I had to deal in numbers. All day. Long days. In Excel models. In financial documents. Literally, everywhere I looked. Luckily, my coworkers didn't initially realize that I was a numbers rookie. Harvard certainly provided good cover. But my suffering was real. I struggled. You might be thinking at this point that the story ends with my genius being discovered, but you would be so wrong.

Also happening at that time were world events. I started the job in 2007, and we all know about the stock market crash in 2008. I should have been panicking about the stocks we were covering, but I couldn't shake my feeling of sadness. How did all these people buy houses they couldn't afford? How did people go from "making it" to "ruined" so suddenly?

There appeared to be no good answer. People were blaming complicated financial instruments called collateralized debt obligations (CDOs). And certainly that was where the problem crystallized. But the underlying issue was much simpler, and I did have an inkling as to how that collapse got started.

> **CDO**
>
> A package of mortgages (many of them bad) that somehow, after packaging, were collectively considered good investments for people to buy into.

I lived in Phoenix, Arizona, from 2002 to 2005, first working as a volunteer and then for two years as a very low-paid nonprofit employee. I will never forget when the city of Tempe, where my nonprofit was based, sent a city employee with glossy folders and a lot of paperwork to our office to, in theory, explain how people like me could buy a house. They talked to me—ME, a $24K per year 23-year-old—about buying a house. Apparently, attending a workshop was the first step in getting into their homebuyer program. But seriously people, even I could do that much math. If I could barely afford rent for the two-bedroom apartment I shared with a roommate, how could I possibly buy a house?

Luckily, I skipped that real estate "opportunity." I remember even after making the decision to not buy the house that mortgage brokers continued to approach me on the street. I would respond that there was no way I could afford them, but they assured me that I could because of how fast the value of the houses could grow and make me rich. Since these interactions were my first adulting years, that seemed normal.

A few years later, I was at my job in Little Rock, dodging Excel spreadsheets left and right. I began to question how this egregious housing collapse had happened when, all at once, it struck me. Maybe those folks who'd lost their homes had never had anyone knowledgeable to help them frame their financial decisions—the lone voice of someone willing to independently give them advice. Many of those housing "advisors" had financial incentives to get people to buy.

Remember those mortgage brokers approaching me? Well, let's think about what happened in the industry that made them more conflicted. Back in the old days, a bank gave a loan for a house and then kept that loan at the bank. They had a vested interest in your ability to afford that house in the first place because if you stopped paying, they lost money. Even more subtly, if you bought a house that was fundamentally unaffordable, they had to keep facing you every time you came in, stressed under the burden of an unaffordable house. But things changed when mortgage brokers got to do something different. They got to help you buy a house with a loan, and then days later they could sell that loan to some massive mortgage company. Then that broker would disappear. They had no responsibility to you, and their incentive was fundamentally misaligned—the faster and bigger you bought, the faster and bigger their payout on a commission.

In this process of learning, I want you to understand that if you feel left out of the industry, it's not you, it's the industry. As the housing crisis warns, you not only have to go it alone, but you should go it alone until you can be sure that people advising you have no conflicts of interest with your best financial interest. People who work in the industry don't do it for free. Everyone needs to make money. By understanding how and how much advisors get paid, you will see that there is no such thing as free advice. When advice is "free," there is a sale being masked as advice. And that sale is likely to be expensive, as those people who lost homes or had their finances ruined in the housing collapse can attest to.

Finally, people weren't buying bigger houses than they could afford as pure investments. Sure, many of those decisions were veiled in that notion, but really, people bought those houses because they wanted them. The brokers were just the conduit to allow a purchase that would have otherwise been impossible. In *Nudge*, Thaler and Sunstein argue that "[g]reed and corruption helped to create the crisis, but simple human frailty played a key role. We will not be able to protect against future crises if we rail against wrongdoers without looking in the mirror and understanding the potentially devastating effects of bounded rationality, self-control problems and social influences."[30]

It is my opinion that the best prevention from falling victim to the next scheme or bubble should probably be one part public policy and two parts education.

Selling and Advising Should Not Be Confused

Thinking about our country's mortgage crisis is what took me down the road of thinking about conflicts of interest for financial advice. What people needed wasn't just someone willing to give them advice, but someone who wasn't trying to make money off them at the same time. And I don't mean free advice. Mortgage brokers love for their clients to think of them as advisors, but what they are offering is a sale—a necessary and good one, if appropriate. Mortgage brokers are good people. I am friends with many of them. But the housing crash proved the point that we can't commingle sales and advice. What people needed then and still need today is non-conflicted advice that positions them at the center of the advisor's motivation.

There are plenty more examples of advice getting mixed up in sales in our industry right now, mix-ups that can have even bigger implications for your money than buying a house. We are seeing it with commissioned insurance brokers or agents who offer complementary financial planning and advice. It's advice that concludes you should buy what they uniquely have to sell (insurance and annuity products).

And there are a lot of young people buying these products.

The issue isn't the sale of the products, and in fact we work with many such insurance brokers to help clients buy term life, disability, car, and homeowners insurance. The difference is that the person making the sale should not also be the person serving as advisor. An advisor should be independently evaluating all your needs and then figuring out what product you should buy in the first place. This centers the focus on you and your best interests.

Why am I talking about this? Well, we keep getting people in our retirement plans who are paying large premiums into whole life policies on themselves, on spouses and, yes, on their kids. Money is finite, and so this means that in many cases it is in lieu of saving into their retirement plans. But what is devastating to me is these people *are* sacrificing to save. They just got advised to buy something that sounded good and smart—by someone who would make money if they bought it or make no money if they didn't buy it.

Take this book. I am selling it to you or someone who wants to buy it for you. Of course, I think this book is great and that you should read it. And of course you can listen to me telling you about what can happen in your life if you read it. You understand that the book costs money because you swipe a credit card or write a check for it. When you do that, you also understand that I will make a piece of the purchase price. That's a pretty clear arrangement. It's a sale in which my role is salesperson.

Now, let's pretend I sit down with you and become your book advisor (we can make this up for now). My role is to independently evaluate all the financial books ever written and suggest the one perfect book for you. Amazingly and coincidentally I produce what? *My book.* I see you shaking your head. That makes no sense. Why do I know that you know that makes no sense? Because you are physically paying money for the book, and you understand I am directly benefiting from the sale. I am too conflicted to be an *advisor* about the best book for you. My advice doesn't seem free or complimentary to you. It seems obviously to be a sale.

When people buy financial products, they usually don't know what the cut is for the broker or agent, or even understand those people get paid at all. This mysterious arrangement knocks you off your game. By pulling back the curtain, I hope to help you stay in play with an awareness of who's benefiting so you can make decisions unclouded by mystery.

Fee-Only Advice Is Less Conflicted Advice, But Still . . .

It used to be that the only mode of employment and income for professionals in the industry was a scenario in which selling commingled with advising. However, a while ago a group of people who wanted to serve in a less conflicted advisory role for clients created a new classification of financial advice, called fee-only advice. This is where the financial advisor commits to not selling anything. Instead, they get paid a percentage of how much money you give them to invest. This is a major improvement.

Still, with fee-only advice, there are two issues:

1. You need mega bucks to get meaningful advice. You probably

count money in dollars or hundreds of dollars, but the advisors count the money their clients give them to manage in thousands. It's no wonder that the average client age for a fee-only advisor is in her 50s, because they are usually the only people with mega bucks.

2. Because they are paid on investments for people who have a lot of money already, fee-only advisors' primary focus is investing, not paying off student loans or credit card debt.

Fee-only advisors pushed the industry forward in a revolutionary way, and they are critical for people in their 50s who might have been good savers but are paralyzed by the notion of having to invest that money. It makes sense that a fee-only advisor has a win-win approach. The client needs that advice and the advisor can make a lot of money providing that service.

But from a global perspective, let's think about the service and its potential to help everyone who needs advice (ahem, like you). Olivia just graduated from college with student loan and credit card debt, with a starting salary at her new job of $45,000. Now would be a super good and critical time to get some advice, but only half of the equation is met. She really could use some financial advice, but the advisor can't make enough money on her. She has no assets from which they can pull a fee.

This arrangement is no one's fault. It's just how the industry has migrated. From your perspective, fee-only advice is not even available to you, since you are probably broke and have more student loans than savings.

I know you might have an instinct to want someone else to handle your money, to hold your hand through major financial decisions, but trust me—you can do this. On your own. But if you ever did want to seek advice and didn't want to be sold something and didn't have assets, take heart. The industry is making another leap.

Fixed-Fee Advising Is the Next Advancement

In 2009, while we were still in the depths of stock market lows, I searched to find whether there was anyone out there giving non-conflicted advice and, through an introduction, found her. I met a woman named Linda Bessette whose business card is quietly passed around town. People knew they could sit on her comfortable brown leather couch in her living room on a quiet street in a quiet neighborhood, and after a couple of hours, understand how to pay off credit card debt or start saving enough for retirement. No investments, no insurance. Just pencil-to-a-yellow-legal-pad did the trick. They wrote a check for those couple of hours, and their lives were thus transformed—by a company that didn't even have a website and couldn't be found in the proverbial Yellow Pages.

Linda Bessette had a generosity and a passion for what she was doing. She didn't see this pesky woman—me, with so many questions— as a competitor. Instead, she knew that for every person who made it to her couch, there were hundreds more who needed to. With the help of Linda, my big idea for a financial business that expanded the simple approach that she was using every day was launched. The mission was this: Create a non-conflicted company where clients can walk in and pay a fixed, hourly fee for independent, non-conflicted advice. More importantly, this would be a place that sells nothing and doesn't require clients to have assets to work with us. We can help clients puzzle through how much house to buy or how much is necessary to save for the kind of retirement they dream of. Then, most importantly, the secret sauce: We'd teach clients to manage their own money in order to pull it all off for themselves.

We named the company "Aptus" which means, quite simply, "appropriate." It was a company built to just do the right thing.

The concept is so simple that when I started the company, I was worried that maybe I was missing something. If charging a fixed fee for advice was so obviously the right way to give financial advice, why wasn't it being done in a widespread way? There's just a lot less money in it because clients are acutely aware of the money they are spending for the advice. How are they aware? Well, they write the check.

For a variety of reasons, including some changes in the industry that educated people on conflicts of interest and the cost of hidden fees, Aptus took off, and the concept of fixed-fee advising is now one of the newest advances in the advisory industry. Not because of us, but coincidentally, many other companies simultaneously have been choosing to charge fixed fees for their advice or money management.

A few years ago we took the fixed-fee concept to company retirement plans, where my team and I got to come face to face with several thousand people and their money. It was these engagements in groups and individual meetings that I met young people like you who just needed a guide through all the jargon and confusion. They would make great, life-changing financial decisions with even a small amount of advice and could avoid the mistakes of credit card debt. They didn't need intensive financial planning. You likely don't need intensive financial planning either.

If you are in that small percentage of people who make a lot of money and have a negative net worth, then you probably need to hire a fixed-fee financial planner to run a financial plan for you, set up various savings vehicles, and then teach you to invest. With a fixed-fee advisor, you will not be in danger of getting sold anything, and you will get a full plan, even if you don't have material savings built up.

But for the majority of you, saving and investing are simple. We are going to walk through the process hand-in-hand. Yes, there is a little math involved, but as it turns out, the most complicated math necessary to master your finances is addition, subtraction, multiplication, and (only in worst-case scenarios) division.

RETIREMENT DREAM TO RETIREMENT REALITY

How good will it feel when you are able to make decisions down the road that you can't even imagine now, like one to leave a job, start a business, give yourself a break during an illness, take a year to write a book, or retire early to pursue a second career in which you don't have to focus so much on income? Or, fill in the blank with your retirement dream. Here's the blank! Go ahead, write it here: _____

_____. If you need extra pages, write more retirement dreaminess in the back of this book. Dream big! Together, we're going to take the steps to make the dream come true, to ensure it becomes a reality—your retirement reality.

As American business magnate and financier T. Boone Pickens famously wrote, "The first billion is the hardest." While most of us can't connect well with that statement, I take his point.

I remember looking at my statements over the first few years of saving and thinking, *These numbers are meager. What's the point?* But over a decade in, I get it. There is a magical moment when you check your accounts, and you realize what all the fuss is about related to money compounding on itself. Your money grows more money, just like the charts I showed you earlier demonstrated. And then that money plus your original money grows even more money.

The first dollars you save are the hardest, so let's rip off the Band-Aid. Realizing that there is this period of time when it will inevitably feel like your savings aren't going anywhere . . . isn't it better to get that over with sooner? Wouldn't you rather feel that in your 20s when you're more flexible and most people your age are going around relatively broke anyway? What about people I work with in their 40s who don't have any money to their name and are feeling the intense heat of non-saving? Worse, what about the woman in her 50s that I mentioned in the introduction who can do little but watch her retirement ship sail into the sunset as we try our best to get a life buoy under her arm? How hard is it to feel both pressure that you should have done something drastic yesterday and the doom of "what's the point" at the same time? Don't do that to your future self.

Trust me, act now. Get that first $1,000 in the account. Then $10,000. Get those hardest dollars into that account, and then it doesn't have to be hard again! You will have ripped off the Band-Aid.

Now, what does ripping look like? Committing to saving can hurt initially, but hold your breath and do it. We typically see double-digit increases in employee savings after we take over retirement plans. Employees sometimes have to downsize homes, cancel gym memberships, scale down vacations, and in general spend less money on things they love in order to make their new savings rates work. I can tell you what it doesn't look like: I sit down with a 26-year-old woman still working her first job out of college, and after pay raises, she is making $40,000. After a conversation with me, she divulges to me that she has so much money left over every month that she doesn't know what to do with it. Ha! Yeah right. That never happens.

This work we are doing to save is easy to execute on a technical level. It is hard at an obvious level—actually parting with money and putting it away into a long-term account. Please dogear this moment we are about to have together. Saving your first dollars from your first paycheck, while technically a sacrifice, certainly doesn't feel the same way because you've never become accustomed to those extras and can find loads of ways to be happy without them. It is much easier to scale up a lifestyle than to scale it down. Imagine if you choose just 10% on your first paycheck in exchange for never having to worry about saving enough for retirement. What do you think? Worth it?

It is. Go to HR today and tell them you want to put 10% of your salary into the company retirement plan. If you work for a company that requires you to wait a few months or even a year before joining the retirement plan, do not panic. Join me in the next chapter so that we can walk through exactly what to do so that you can pay yourself first while waiting.

STEP 1: PAY YOURSELF FIRST

I want you to save 10% for retirement. I want you to pay yourself first. This only requires one decision, one time; you do not have to obsess on the issue. You do not have to be responsible in any other part of your life, but I want you to do it here. This may be the best decision you ever make.

If you don't know where to go to sign up for your plan, please call your HR department or the person in your company who handles your paycheck. This is where retirement plans are administered. They might hand you to a financial firm to get signed up, and that is okay. Companies outsource the administration of their retirement plans to other companies, so they may give you login instructions or even a paper sign-up with a financial institution's name at the top. Fill it out, and know that you can and should ask questions on any part of the sign-up that is confusing to you. Thaler and Sunstein highlight a study analyzing the time people spent making these massive life decisions on retirement. "Fifty-eight percent spent less than one hour determining both their contribution rate and investment decisions. Most people spend more time than that picking a new tennis racket or television set."[31] When I speak to groups, I ask them if they think that they've collectively spent more time picking their retirement savings rate than any one person in the group spent picking their last car. The group always shakes their head no.

Your retirement account savings rate decision is more important than the car, the house, the tennis racket, or the car insurance. Please give it the same love you might give all of those other things. Given the confusing nature of retirement plans, I encourage you to ask many questions so that you can make great decisions.

Here are the questions that I would ask if I were signing up. Feel free to just go on and ask them, but I will address them below as well.

1. How much should I save at my age?

2. What is the company's match? What is the vesting schedule?

3. Should I choose the traditional retirement plan or the Roth?

4. Which investment fund(s) should I choose?

5. Will the investment fund change over time on its own, or will I be responsible for doing that?

How Much Should Olivia Save?

Back to our friend, Olivia. We are rewriting her story, and at this moment she is a college grad about to make $45,000. First, she was planning on a few last hurrah post-graduation trips. We get to her before she puts trips on that credit card. But now she is about to go to her first day on the job. She is about to make the most important life decision—how much to save.

Recall that she is 23, and she is part of the lucky group of college grads who get this simple message to save 10% early in life. (She is also part of the lucky group that has a job at all as pandemic grads barrel into devastating unemployment numbers.) Like Olivia, if you are in your 20s, the number you should enter into the blank for your retirement is 10%. Later, I will discuss a slight (and temporary) modification to this very clear number to take into consideration student loan or credit card debt. The savings is calculated based on the percentage you choose times your gross pay, and it comes out typically every pay period. Olivia makes $45,000 per year, and gets paid every other week. This means she gets paid 26 times per year. If we divide $45,000 by 26 we get $1,730.77. That is her "gross" pay at every paycheck, or in other words that is her contractual pay from the company, before the federal and state governments, health insurance company, parking deck, and others get their hands on pieces of her paycheck. Her savings rate would be 10% times $1,730.77 = $173.08 per paycheck. On a monthly basis, it adds up to $375.

In other words, we are going to skim the first $173 out of her first paycheck as it goes into the funnel to ensure that Olivia is paying herself first.

Pay Yourself First

Action item

Call HR and have them contribute 10% of your gross pay to your retirement account. If you're self-employed, open a Roth IRA.

There is a hard way to do this and an easy way. The hard way is to ask Olivia to save *after* she got into credit card debt and took on the car loan. Or even the things she became comfortable buying and enjoying on $45,000. Finding $173.08 in her paycheck at that point would feel insurmountable. And, believe me, I have sat in the meetings with the person trying to figure out if they can afford to save. There is usually a long pause, back of the envelope math, and lots of thinking and worrying about how to make that work. Why? Because most of us pretty much adapt to whatever our paycheck is, whether it's $45,000 per year or $450,000 per year. We can adapt up or down, but you might guess it is far easier to do the "adapt up" thing.

Now for the easy way. Olivia sits down on her first day on the job and checks the box to save, filling in 10%. Like Olivia, maybe you happen to be reading this before you start your job OR before a newly-awarded raise hits your paycheck. If so, cha-ching. Go sign up on day one. Make sure you never see a paycheck without your retirement money already coming out. You will not know the difference. I promise!

Could you use that money that you're putting toward your retirement right now instead? Yes, absolutely. Can anyone ever *not* use more money? I love to spend money, and I always have a list of things I desperately want to spend money on. It's hard and painful for me not to use the money I save for the things I want so badly. Mostly, I love to do charitable giving, but I also want new clothes (more than the new clothes I already bought), to redecorate my house, and, shoot, okay, I admit I would sure love to buy a Tesla right now. I make a lot more money than I used to in my 20s. Back then, the things on my wish list were being able to eat out, join a fancier gym, and drive a nice(er) car. Check, check, check. I can do all those things, but they didn't satiate my brain. My brain's wishlist grew alongside my husband's and my profit from our businesses. If it hasn't already, your brain's wishlist will grow alongside yours.

A dear friend who is truly a fashionista and loves buying clothes has worked hard to get on a good cash management system. She told me something that proves the point. Right now, she desperately wants $500 to spend on a few pieces she has been drooling over for a few weeks. But she said that if someone handed her $5,000 to go spend on clothes, she would spend it and then have a list of even more she would want to buy.

Remember the irrational consumer argument above? That's the game playing out in the heads of most *Homo sapiens*. While our name means "wise humans," sometimes we remain captive to brains that won't switch off our hunter/gatherer ancestry—the "gather and eat all you can while you can because it could go away and you will have missed your chance" messages are still flowing. A piece of our brains will always convince us that we need to buy just a thing or two more and then life will be complete. It has us convinced we can shut it up if we just go buy that one more thing.

It's a trap. We will never have enough money. We will only ever feel satiated by a purchase for a flash, if at all. Anytime you find yourself justifying a purchase to appease the brain, just know it's a lie. Your brain will never stop asking for more.

The point is that you might as well save. If you save from the beginning, then you only have to deal with the pain of knowing the opportunity cost of your money. You know you are saving *at the cost of* spending on that one more thing. But, let me tell you, that is so much easier than saving when you actually have to *end* spending on that one more thing you are already enjoying. Ouch.

My partners and I witness people making this decision. All. Day. Long. Every day. We deal with people who either start saving enough from the beginning or have to start saving mid-course. As of right now, saving from the beginning is not as common, but it is a thing of beauty. The thing we have observed with these people (keeping in mind that I am not one of them) is that they don't think it's a big deal. When I meet one of these young people with a large retirement already accumulated, I mention how cool it is. They just shrug. They don't understand that it is actually hard for people who haven't saved from the beginning to start saving. It's a bigger deal, but the saver just doesn't understand that. Another observation is that I have never met someone saving a certain percentage who told me they *wanted* to start saving less. I have never met a single retiree who regretted how much they had saved over the years.

The more common situation is someone who is undersaving. For them, and this might be you, changes have to be made and changes can cause varying degrees of pain. I love it when someone is undersaving only by a small amount. For them, eating out a little less, not getting quite as many manicures, or scaling down the vacations is enough to make it work. They rip off the Band-Aid, and sometimes the pull is so subtle that they don't yelp. They simply adapt to it, much the way one adapts to a higher health insurance premium or a car payment.

For others, the adjustment is more significant. A major lifestyle change is involved, like moving into a smaller home or switching to a more modest car. I can tell you that these folks struggle mightily to get to a decision. They don't want to move from the house they love or they worry about how it might look to outsiders if they bought a smaller house. Would they still feel successful to themselves and appear successful to others?

The car situation is always interesting to me. Buying later model cars is not usually necessary. Cars last so long, so when we are buying the late model car there is usually a lot more cool factor than safety factor weighing into the decision. Michelle Singletary is hilariously clear on the topic when she says, "You are not what you drive! And you should not care about what anybody thinks about the kind of car you have. I have a car that's so old, if somebody hits my car, I don't know if it's your dent or my dent. And that's because my money is being put toward things that are going to increase my net worth or help my family."[32]

Most of the time, you are far better off paying for repairs, even costly ones, every year than buying a newer car. If you find yourself justifying a later model car over making repairs, do the math first. Add up the cost of a newer car for one year. Then, add up the average repairs you have made in the past year or two and what you could reasonably expect to make over the next year with your current car. Most of the time, the math tilts in favor of keeping your car.

What I think many people starting careers deal with is the need to look and act the part of successful. I heard one such anecdote from a recent college graduate. She is brilliant and driven—finishing college in three and a half years. She landed a nationally competitive job, but even she struggles with finding the right balance. How much does driving the right car or wearing the right clothes add to a perception of success? Could that perception lead to even greater success? I don't know the answer, but I do know that pressure to look successful doesn't get better. It actually gets worse as people try to make partner, land deals, and start businesses. They feel the need to spend more than they would otherwise to look the part—maybe even to convince themselves they deserve the part. But that can come at a significant cost down the road. My best advice is to try hard not to succumb to those pressures early in life if you can avoid them.

My husband drives a nice truck, and I drive a late model minivan. (I hope I didn't just lose you. It does sport this bumper sticker: "I used to be cool.") We live in a nice house and enjoy our nice house. Remember, I promised you early on that deprivation is not the goal. You can certainly aspire to nicer cars and homes. But what I am seeing in my meetings is young people who buy those things when they are young, before getting to the right savings rate, before paying off the student loans and credit card debt, and before knowing what can really bring joy, like travel, dining out with friends, or entertainment. Then when the credit card debt starts to pile up, stress ensues.

These are your questions to wrestle with. I wrestle with them every day. But I have something that you don't have: the benefit of hearing others wrestle with them every day. I get to see wonderful people in front of me, with amazing friends, amazing kids, and amazing lives, struggling with the image that they want to maintain. It is far more complicated for them internally than what people see externally. When I can see so clearly that they should sell the house and downsize, or they should keep driving the older car, or they should stop buying so many clothes, I am always intrigued when they can't do it. I see myself in so many people, especially my former self that lived that stress. While the answer seems so simple from far away, I also understand that it's not so simple on the ground.

I see the power that our consumer culture has over us (as we will discuss later). Those items might not just be preventing them from saving, they may be adding to credit card debt. On my side, the answer is so simple. Just stop. Get off that hamster wheel. Your life will be much happier on the other side—the side without the credit card debt hanging over you or the knowledge that you have nothing to show for all that day after day, month after month, year after year, hard work. Shut everything else out, close your eyes for a minute, and imagine the pain of knowing that you pay everyone else first and leave nothing, NOTHING, for yourself after all that. Really allow yourself to see it in your mind's eye and to feel it in your body. Not good. You don't want to be that version of yourself. You don't want to do that to yourself.

I don't want to do that to myself. I am the lucky one—the spender, the one still tempted day after day to spend, who witnesses people in real pain. I comfort them with an easy fix—spend just a little less, and you will be a lot happier. These constant reminders keep me in line, dedicated to paying myself first and sticking to the cash management system I will walk you through later. And now, I personally reap the rewards of the years of saving to date, enough to identify the feeling evoked by Farnoosh Torabi's definition: "Wealth doesn't have to be a mansion. It can just be moving your schedule around without financial consequence that you value much more."[33]

Luckily, I have seen a whole lot of people downsize, and not one time, not in one single case, have they ever regretted it or changed course. Remember, if you cut back your lifestyle, you always have the choice to ramp it back up. But people rarely do because they usually realize it wasn't making them as happy as they were giving it credit for anyway—not as happy as the security they traded it for. One woman who had been in significant credit card debt and spent two years slaying it told me that there was not one thing she could purchase or one vacation she could go on that would be worth the return to the way she had felt before. She was enduring that stress and anxiety year after year, yet after making the commitment, she wouldn't agree to feel it even for one more day, ever again. That is powerful.

You have another option. Let's say you are reading this book and mostly agree with me that saving now makes sense, but you decide to consciously kick the can down the road. What IF you went into credit card debt for this upcoming wedding? Shoot, everyone does it. Your friends do it, your parents might have done it, and credit is everywhere just waiting for you to use it to collect points, miles, and cash back. What if you just got in a little financial trouble, just lived a little? Don't you have the right to do it?

Yes! You can! You can certainly learn it the way most of us older folks had to learn it. But we would all tell you that if we could go back, we would have all done it differently. This is one area of life where there is no getting away with it; that decision, and the trouble it leads to, is a boulder chained to your ankle. Once you strap it on, it's going to be awfully hard to walk forward. So you might think twice before clasping that ankle bracelet and instead send the boulder rolling down the nearest hill.

Making major financial mistakes no longer has to be a rite of passage for adulthood.

How much does it cost not to make major financial mistakes? If you are in your 20s, and you are convinced, then for you the answer to how much to save is 10%. Boom! Now, put that in the box for savings percentage in your retirement plan. Let's say you are in your 30s and haven't started saving just yet. You probably need to commit somewhere between 12–15%. If you are in your 40s and never saved, consider 20%–25%, and if you are in your 50s, believe it or not—sorry—that needs to be 30%–40%.

Thankfully for you in your 50s, while that would call for an extreme lifestyle change, you know that retirement is so close you can taste it. You know that a lifestyle change even more extreme would be coming soon, anyway—so why not make a smaller one now? These numbers look scary, I know they are, but I'm begging you not to keep ignoring them. As you are growing a little more tired of work than you were in the last decade and can more readily imagine one day wanting to stop doing that work altogether, there is still an opportunity to have the retirement you want. Doing some dreaming of the life in retirement that you're closer to actually realizing may be the motivation you need to make some big changes. This is your wakeup call, and it's time to do what you can where you can. Since this book is geared toward women aged 18 to 30, hopefully those of you in that age bracket can see these percentages as a harbinger of where you will be if you don't act now. Let them serve as motivation to put that 10% in the box and throw yourself an "I totally love me/I am awesome" party.

Do Not Wait.

Whatever your age bracket, let's say you are all aboard and ready to write in that number. Unfortunately, if you work for a small company, you might be facing a savings killer—the waiting period, which I referenced earlier. This is a period of time that some companies want you to work for them before you are eligible for the retirement plan. A typical waiting period for small companies is one year. This means you would not be able to save into the plan during that time. That's not ideal because after a year, you've gotten used to the size of your paycheck!

If you have any kind of waiting period to join your retirement plan, even three months, no problem. You have the opportunity to do something critical. Prevent yourself from adapting to living off your entire paycheck by saving 10% somewhere else, and treat it as savings that you never plan to spend. Set up a savings account at your bank, or maybe even at a bank other than the one you use, and that will be the start of your important emergency fund. Since this is a pile of cash you will never spend, opening that particular savings account at a different bank than the one you use can reduce temptation to spend it.

Some small companies will even have relationships with credit unions or local banks to facilitate saving for employees. Ask. You can start there, and that is the easiest path. You might even be able to set it up at the company if they have their own credit union. If not, there are easy online savings accounts you can set up that pay pretty good interest rates, like Ally Bank or American Express. The point is, you don't want your emergency savings connected to your main checking account. Mark my words: You will spend it! Once you set up the account, I want you to calculate 10% of your gross pay per pay period, and then ask payroll to deposit that amount into your emergency savings account every pay period.

While, yes, it's great to have the pile of cash accumulate into your emergency fund over that waiting period, that's the lesser point. The bigger point is that when it is time to join the retirement plan, you will not have to reduce your pay or lifestyle to do it. You will not run the risk that when the time comes, contributing 10% would be too painful, leaving you to not do it or to save too little.

Again, let's do the calculation together, using the same pay of $45,000. $45,000 x 10% = $4,500 per year. But let's say in your case you don't get paid every other week. Instead you get paid twice a month on the 1st and 15th (24 payments per year). To save 10% of 45,000 is $4,500 per year. You would ask payroll to withdraw $187 ($4,500 divided by 24) per pay period and deposit that money into your emergency fund.

Then, once you have become newly eligible for the retirement plan, end or reduce the emergency fund contributions and start saving 10% into the retirement plan. Your paycheck will not know the difference, and neither will you. Oh, and at the same time, after one year you would have $4,500 saved! Wow!

What Is the Company's Match or Contribution?

I love free money. Do you love free money? I promise you will love free money. Free money is fabulous. And that is exactly what a company puts into your retirement account when they have a retirement match.

Can you believe this? We have hidden the coolest feature of a retirement plan behind the dumbest description ever—the company match. The match is not a dating feature at your company. No, it is your company saying they are so excited for you to save that they will reward you for it.

Your company might also have an outright fixed contribution, a profit-sharing contribution based on the performance of the company, or a combination of two or all three of these (match, fixed contribution, and/or profit-sharing contribution).

Save 10% of your income, regardless of match. The company match, while incredible (free money!) has been an unwitting killer of saving enough for retirement, and I will explain. How many times has someone proudly walked up to me and said they were "maxing out their retirement plan?" Ninety-nine times out of 100, I know they are mistaken. They are not maxing out their retirement, because in 2020 that would be contributing $19,500 to their plan. That's the federal limit for how much you can legally contribute—how much you can actually "max." But if you are making $45,000 a year, you are probably not maxing out your retirement plan. That would be pretty difficult.

Instead, they are often maxing out the match. Let's get to what a retirement match often looks like. Most companies have what is called a "Safe Harbor" match. (Again—can you believe how confusing these words are? Who came up with that phrase?) In a Safe Harbor match, the company agrees to add, dollar for dollar, what you put into the retirement plan up to 3%, then on your next 2% of contributions it will put in $0.50 on the dollar. In other words, doing the math, if you put in 3% they will put in 3%. If you put in 4%, they will put in 3.5%. If you put in 5%, they will put in 4%. If you put in 6%, they will put in 4%. If you put in 7%, they will put in, wait—starting to see the pattern here. They are still just putting in 4%?

So, I should just put in 5% to maximize my free money? Ugh, it sounds so much like the right thing to do, but it is indeed *not* the right thing to do. The language, the language, the language! It all is either nonsensical or misleading. Who came up with this stuff!?! "Maxing out the match" is such a misleading statement because it provides you an artificial limit.

Here is the psychology of "maxing out the match." With pensions disappearing, some companies that still feel a sense of responsibility in this area have been desperate to get their employees to save anything. Believe it or not, they care about their employees and would never want people to work for them all of their lives and then at the end of it not be able to stop working, or worse, stop working into poverty. One of the ways they encourage their employees to save is by offering a match. This way, if an employee at least saves 5%, that person will collect all the free money on the table. As a society, we are looking at the retirement crisis and wanting people to do at least something, the bare minimum, but that something or bare minimum is not going to result in a full, on-time retirement. It is simply "something." It is not, however, enough.

Do you see the distinction? I love free money, and we can log in to our accounts periodically and marvel at the acceleration of our retirement accounts from this free money. But to be clear, the match that a company makes should not impact how much money you deposit. If you are aged 18 to 30, you should put in 10%, regardless of what the company is doing.

Some companies are seeing the importance of anchoring their employees at appropriate savings rates to address chronic undersaving, and they are implementing "stretch" matches. These are matches that might be lower on the front end (instead of dollar-for-dollar, they might be $0.50 per dollar), but they "stretch" out over high percentages. For instance, they could match 50% of what you put in up to 10%. If you put in 10%, then they put in 5%. But if you only put in 5%, then the company only puts in 2.5%. You would be crazy to contribute anything less than 10%. In this case "maxing the match" to get all the free money means you're being rewarded for hitting that magical 10% savings rate. *That* is a beautiful match right there. Can't you just see my eyes sparkling?

There are other types of employer contributions, like profit sharing or nonelective contributions, which are pure gravy. You don't have to put anything in, and the company just contributes some amount into the account. You can't control it. You just enjoy free money piling into your account and helping your stash grow. Again, regardless of these contributions, you would still put in 10%.

The most common mistake people make when they hear the message to "Save 10" is they calculate the match with their contribution. I will get people saying they save 10% because they put in 6%, and then with the Safe Harbor match, the company puts in 4%. Well, that's not gonna get you to retire. The best way to explain it is this. A lot of people ask me what the "number" is that they should shoot for to retire. What number does the average person need to hit before they can walk off the job? Sadly, it's not that simple. Your ability to retire is a ratio of what you have saved divided by what you need to spend every year. An easy estimate that should work for most people and in most economic environments is that your retirement nest egg should be about 25 times the amount of your annual spending. Let's say you spend $60,000 the year before you retire. Then you would need to have

$60,000 x 25, or $1.5 mil. in a retirement account. So, the smaller your bottom number is relative to your big number, or vice versa, the better your chances to retire. When you are saving 10%, just as importantly as you are putting that money into an account, you are also reducing your lifestyle by 10%. That reduced lifestyle over time is what gets your bottom number lower and able to let your retirement dollars last longer.

Olivia has been saving for two years. She pulls up her retirement account and sees that it is $10,000—definitely not enough to retire. But is she on track? (I used the Vanguard Retirement Income Calculator,[34] which you could pull up and follow along if you want to see whether you are on track or what it would take to get there.) For Olivia, I made the following assumptions: 25-year old planning to retire at 65, making $45,000 per year, saving 10% (with the company match is saving 14%), with $10,000 already saved, needing to replace 80% of income, expecting an annual rate of return of 5% and a monthly social security income (in today's dollars) of $1,756, derived from using the Social Security Quick Calculator[35] for a guesstimate. Entering in that data, the calculator shows that the monthly dollars needed in retirement would be $3,000 and that the monthly income from social security and retirement savings is estimated to be a little more than that. Looks like someone is poised to retire one day.

Let's assume a small change to make our point. The woman in our example saves 6% and has an employer match of 4%. Again, she's 25-years-old, planning to retire at 65, making $45,000 per year, saving 10% (between her 6% and her employer match of 4%), with $8,500 already saved, expecting an annual rate of return of 5% and a social security income (in today's dollars) of $1,756. Remember how she needed to replace 80% of her income before? Well, that is reflecting the fact that she no longer needed to save 10%, but still needed to pay social security and medicare taxes, a very small federal/state tax, and her home mortgage. Those things are all the same now, except she is saving 6% of *her money*, so her lifestyle is 4 percentage points higher. We now go into the Vanguard Income Calculator and nudge that 80% up to 84% to reflect the 4 percentage points of lifestyle. Now, we see she would have $2,729 monthly available to spend but she would probably need about $3,150, a roughly $400 gap. She would either have to spend less on things she enjoys in retirement or work longer, all things being equal.

The precise outcome for her wealth is uncertain. The market could grow her money faster than we predict and it could all work out. It could also grow slower. The point is that such a small change that would be barely noticeable on the savings end could end up with a pronounced impact on the retirement end.

The final risk is one that should be familiar to the younger generations, from millennials to Gen Z-ers. Often, employees are not staying in jobs long enough to become fully "vested" in the company's match. Let's say that Olivia had a different match than the scenario we ran. That was a Safe Harbor match with the great perk of being fully vested, meaning that from the beginning, the employee "owns" every dollar the company puts in immediately. Now Olivia has a new deal where the company puts in 50% of what she contributes up to 7%. To get to 10% between her contribution and the match would mean she puts in 7%, and the company puts in 3.5%. The company has a vesting schedule called

Vesting

The percentage of the employer contribution to your retirement account that you "own." You are always 100% vested in your own contributions.

"cliff" vesting. She would have to work there three years to "own" all those contributions the company made into her retirement plan. If she changed jobs any time before working there for three years, she would forfeit all the contributions the company made to her account. If she persisted in having a chronic savings rate of 7% her whole life, then at 65 she could find herself short and unable to stop working at that age.

This is why I want you to understand how important it is that you save the right amount into your retirement plan, almost regardless of what the company is contributing.

I recommend that you play with the Vanguard Calculator or any readily available retirement calculator and remember that we don't have a crystal ball for the future. If you think a 5%-6% return on your money is too optimistic considering market volatility, then pull the dial back. You can then increase your savings rate to compensate for the lower return. Again, we have no crystal ball and can't predict the market, so it's important to be fully aware this is "play"—a good tool but still a guessing game. Think social security is going away? (I don't, for the record.) Then don't put a social security assumption in there. Again, adjust your savings rate up accordingly. Also, if you have a salary that is double or triple the $45,000 you will find that the numbers get harder, as social security has less of an impact in terms of contributions and benefits on higher wage earners. You will see that 10% might not be enough to save to have the retirement you imagine. Maybe at your first job you need to do something more like 15%+.

Of course there are always caveats. If you have a robust pension plan or a really high savings match percentage that is immediately vested, then maybe there could be some wiggle room. I just say, wow, that's great that someone else is putting so much money into my retirement, as well, but I don't leave anything up to chance. I will save my 10% and accept the burden of accidentally having too many options for fun things to do like travel, participate in expensive hobbies, or have the actual option to retire early.

To recap, I want you to save 10% of your income, regardless of the match. Look at the match as a saving accelerator, nothing more. It should not have a bearing on how much you save.

Vesting Schedule

Let's go back to the vesting schedule that determines when your contribution from the company, via a match or any contribution, is fully yours. The company's money does get deposited into your account, and you get to invest it the way you want. But until you have worked at the company for a period of time, that money is not fully yours.

I don't want to spend a lot of time on this because it is complicated and unnecessary to think about. Not many people take, leave, or stay in jobs because of vesting schedules. There are two common types of vesting schedules. The first we described above, a cliff vest, where after 3 years whatever the company has contributed so far and ongoing into the future is 100% yours. But, if you work there fewer than 3 years, none of it is. The other most common vest is a graded vesting schedule over 6 years. Essentially the first 2 years you don't own anything, then after 2 years it is 20%, 3 years 40%, 4 years 60%, 5 years 80%, and then 100% at the end of 6 years.

In the end, it just doesn't matter. A match is not why you are saving. The company's contribution is not why you are saving. You are saving for your retirement. And while I do think a vest should be one consideration in staying versus leaving a company, and if you are close to a significant increase and not in major pain you might think of sticking around, in the end, you have to pursue your career ambitions.

So, on the list of things to think or worry about or understand the most, this one's a blah. You can cross it off the list, but at least you know what it is and won't get tripped up when the HR representative or retirement plan advisor talks about it.

What is important to know is that you are 100% "vested" in every contribution YOU make. That is your money, and when you leave you get to take it all. There is no risk in that.

You Can't Beat the Tax Benefit of This Plan Combined With Automation

There is nowhere to save that is going to help you retire like your company retirement plan. Even taking away the free money element, it is still the best thing you will ever have.

The federal government, first of all, is making quite the deal with you. Either get a tax deduction immediately on your contributions and pay taxes later in retirement, *or* take the tax hit now on your contributions and never pay taxes again. This decision is So. Much. Fun. You are getting to make a really big decision that's a win either way—the bet is just which is going to be a bigger win. We'll get to that in a second.

Next, automation is amazing. You make the decision to save, and you get to automate the process of saving and the tax benefit. You get to put small chunks of money into an account, invest those chunks, and your money just accumulates over your lifetime—without having to think about it.

I would love to sit down with the man who decided to name retirement plans after their lines in the tax code. Hey, for-profit company, let's name your retirement plans 401(k)s! Hey nonprofits, I've been up all night thinking of the perfect, most inspiring name for the employees who are passionate about changing the world—403(b)s! Oh, and for the public servants, have I got an account name fit for a mayor—the 457(b)!

Let's take a second to think of a better name for these. How about "Retirement Plan?" "Future Fund?" "Freedom Fund?" Come on. Surely we can crowdsource a name that merits the beauty and importance of what is happening.

On that note, what is, exactly, happening with this line in the tax code?

Roth 401(k), 403(b), and 457(b)

Let's first take a second to understand taxes. You will pay a handful of taxes every pay period, and they are a percentage of what you make, the biggest being your federal taxes.

For Olivia as a single filer, as of 2020, the first $9,875 she makes is taxed at 10%. After deductions, if she made exactly $9,875, then she would pay $987 that year. Anything over that up to $40,125 is then taxed at 12%. Anything over that up to $85,525 is taxed at 22%. And so on. She pays less in taxes on her first dollars than her last dollars as the tax rate gets progressively higher. So, to figure out what she would pay is to add up taxes at each tax bracket along the way.

The brackets are different for married couples. For instance, as of 2020, if you are married, the first $19,750 you make is taxed at 10%. Anything over that up to $80,250 is then taxed at 12%. Anything over that up to $171,050 is taxed at 22%.

You will also have social security tax and Medicare taxes that come out of your check, and many people also have state taxes. These taxes add up and can take a lot of money out of your check.

Here's the thing. Yours might not be that much (comparatively). After deductions, which lower your income in the eyes of the government, you might not actually pay much of anything via income taxes. In that case, you have the option to do something super cool called a Roth 401(k)/403(b)/457(b). The Roth option allows you to save into the retirement plan without the tax deduction now (meaning, you will pay taxes on what you put into the Roth account for which you cannot claim a deduction), but you will never pay taxes again on that money. Let's repeat—you will never, ever pay taxes on the money. It can grow and grow and grow in the market, and then at the end you don't have to pay taxes on the growth of the money at all. Psychologically, Roth money in retirement is a thing of beauty. When you look at your Roth account, you know that what you see is what you get. You don't have to constantly factor in the cost of taxes that reduce the balance in retirement.

So what's the difference between the Roth option in your retirement plan and the traditional, or "pre-tax" option? Maybe Roth makes the most sense now, but let me explain why one day when you are making more money, you will likely want to switch.

Pre-Tax, or Traditional 401(k), 403(b), or 457(b)

Enter the world's best way to dodge the biggest tax—the income tax. If you put money into your retirement plan, you get to take those dollars off the top of your heap. You get to take the most expensively taxed dollars off the top and deposit them into your retirement plan. WOW! Let's say within 10 years, Olivia is in management at her company making $120,000. She is well into the 24% marginal federal tax bracket. Assuming she pays state income tax of 6%, that gets her to nearly 30% in marginal taxes, or taxes on her last, incremental dollars earned. Can you imagine giving 30 cents on every incremental dollar you make? Let's say Olivia is still saving 10%, which on $120,000 would be $12,000 in a year. This means she would get to dodge $12,000 x 30%, or $3,600 in taxes! Just by putting $12,000 of her paycheck into HER retirement accounts, she gets to avoid paying all those taxes. Put another way, if she put $12,000 into her retirement plan, she will only *feel* $8,400 coming out of her check. Put an even better way, the government is giving her a huge opportunity to stretch her finite dollars, to save in a way that is less painful because she won't feel the full brunt of saving. Wow.

Now, let's get real. The government wants and needs its money, and you will pay them—eventually. Here is the deal you are making: Don't make me pay taxes on the dollars I contribute to my retirement plan, and you (government) can hit me up later for those Benjamins in retirement. Every time I take the money out to spend it, I promise to pay income taxes on what I take out.

But, remember the marginal tax brackets? Whereas in your early life when you are presumably making more money than when you are retired (retirement being, like, not working), you can probably expect to have less income. Every time you take money out of the retirement plan, it's considered income, as if you are working. And you get taxed on that income, like you are working. The caveat is whereas you took the *top* dollars off the table to save, your income from retirement explores the marginal tax brackets from the *bottom up.*

In other words, you can probably expect to pay less on your dollars in taxes in your retirement years than you saved on your dollars in working years when you were making a lot of money. THAT is the tax deal. This matters. A lot of people go through their lives not understanding the magnitude of how much this matters, and they lose the chance to make this incredible deal with the government which will help them stretch dollars and be able to save more than they would otherwise.

This brings me back to the industry and something I have had clients recount to me. How do people end up buying these insurance and annuity products in lieu of saving into retirement plans? They don't understand how the policies work, but they remember thinking it was a good idea when the guy first explained it to them. To make the initial $200 monthly premium payment, clients temporarily backed down retirement contributions. But 10 years later, they still hadn't gotten around to increasing the contribution.

Here's one thing for sure. If they had kept money accumulating in the retirement plan, the salesperson would have made zero dollars for his friendly "financial planning" help. The first year they paid those monthly $200 premiums, he made 100% of those in commission, or $2,400. Whaaaaaaat??? The next 10 years, depending on his structure, he probably made $240 annually—for doing nothing. Tell me who is getting on track here.

The point is that there is not a single place better than your retirement plan—not real estate, not forex trading, not whole life policies, not annuities—to save, grow, and secure your future. The simplest, easiest, most convenient way to save happens to be the best financial bang for your buck. Anyone inviting you to a free steak dinner, a free lunch, or a free financial planning session likely has a lot to gain personally from you getting talked out of your money, your precious savings. Ladies—there is no such thing as a free lunch.

So what's your retirement saving number? Is it 10%? Great. You can download our worksheet at ButFirstSave10.com to proudly enter your savings number at the top and then follow along to get the rest of your numbers to make that savings rate work.

"Pay Yourself First" Financial Plan

1. Pay Yourself First: Retirement Savings & Debt Reduction

Gross pay x_____% retirement savings and debt reduction rate

= $_____

NET PAY = $_____ / MONTH

Saving for Retirement When You Have Credit Card Debt

I am not sure about a lot of things in the world of investing, but in the world of saving I am absolutely positive that saving into your company retirement plan is the best choice you can make. It is the closest to pounding the table I can get, but sadly, there is one piece of gray area. That is debt.

If you have loads of debt or some high-interest debt, then your best option might be to contribute into your company retirement plan to get your free money via the company retirement "match," if they have one, and then use the rest of your savings rate to aggressively pay off the debt. At Aptus, we advise about this a lot in our retirement plans. With Olivia, we were using the example of someone just starting a career in her 20s. Let's say you picked up this book at 29 years old, making $60,000 per year, and have $10,000 in credit card debt at a 24% interest rate. Lots of hands just went up. You are not alone.

Your retirement plan has the Safe Harbor match I explained earlier. In your case, since you have not started saving yet *and* have a lot of debt, I would recommend at least a 15% savings rate to put toward savings and excess debt repayment. The first 5% of that savings rate would ideally go to get your "free" money via the match. Then the next 10% would go toward your debt. On a monthly basis, that means that $250 per month would go into retirement, and then $500 per month would be allocated to your various credit card bills as "extra" payments. In other words, your minimum payments should be treated as bills and come out of your basic monthly cash flow, and the $500 would be allocated toward either the highest interest credit card or to get the smallest balances out of the way (the debt snowball).

> **Cash Flow**
>
> The money from your paycheck that hits your checking account after all taxes, benefits, and retirement contributions are taken out.

By allocating some of your savings rate to debt repayment, you would have your credit cards paid off in a little under two years. Then the $500 you were already paying on debt gets transferred into your retirement savings (the full 15% savings rate going toward your retirement). More importantly, remember those minimum payments? Now that you're debt-free, that's money you can spend as your reward. (Lifestyle increase!)

Debt Snowball

The process of paying off the smallest balance credit cards or other forms of debt. When that small balance is paid off, the payment you used to pay then gets applied to the next smallest debt. And that continues until all the debt is repaid.

The debt snowball is a much-debated phenomenon. The math doesn't make sense. It always makes sense to pay off the highest interest debt first because then you pay less in interest during the time you pay off the debt. The debt snowball might add a month or two of payments to your length of debt paydown since your higher debt balances might also carry the highest interest rate, thus growing your debt relatively faster while you pay it off.

The argument for the snowball is the psychological win that comes earlier when you can physically reduce your number of debts. I once heard a Q&A with personal finance expert Naseema McElroy of Financially Intentional. She was asked by an audience member why she recommends a debt snowball over paying off the highest interest rate debt first. Her witty response, "Math didn't get you into this mess. It's probably not going to get you out of it." Meaning, the thrill of buying things gets us into debt; the thrill of seeing debt go away will keep us motivated to pay it all off.

Either way, you do you. I am just cheering from the wings.

Saving for Retirement When You Have Student Loan Debt

Enter any room of 18- to 30-year-olds and ask, "Who has student loan debt?" The hands will shoot up. Ladies, we have student loan debt and a lot of it. We have more of it than men, in fact. And research shows that it affects our ability to save. Interestingly enough, the difference between a large student loan balance and a small student loan balance will not have a proportionate effect on saving.[36] Let's say you have $5,000 in student loan debt or $75,000 in student loan debt. According to the research, in either case you are so scared of the debt that you don't want to save until it is gone. Alarmingly, just the *presence* of the student loan debt impacts our saving habits!

If you have a student loan plan, and it is a good one—meaning you spent a good couple hours understanding your student loan debt and which repayment program makes the most sense to get them paid off, or even better, get some of them forgiven—then you will have to figure out what makes the most sense on the balance between saving for retirement and paying off the student loans. Just think it through. Are you on a 20-year repayment plan through one of the income-driven repayment programs? Would it make sense to wait 20 years to get to your appropriate savings rate for retirement? No way. If you are in your 20s and are in a long student loan repayment program—which could absolutely be the right choice—then you have to save 10% into your retirement plan. You can't afford to wait 20 years.

If you work for a 501(c)3, and assuming that the program has not been cancelled (it was not cancelled as of the publishing of this book in summer 2020), then you must consider the Public Student Loan Forgiveness Program (PSLF). Assuming you don't make much money, you would pay less than a 10-year, monthly repayment based on an affordability factor the federal government has set. At the end of 10 years, whatever amount you didn't pay over all that time just gets wiped clean.

Yes, I know, 99% of people who applied to have their loans forgiven last year were denied. Persevere. Those were folks who didn't have qualifying loans, didn't get in the right program, had their heads buried in the sand, or didn't make qualifying payments. A lot more people in 2022 should be eligible for this forgiveness, and that's when we will see the program start taking effect. But here's the deal. If you think you might qualify, meaning you have federal Stafford or other types of federal loans and you work for a nonprofit, then you need to be on top of this. You need to be certifying your time working for the nonprofit.

You need to be in the best student loan program there is. Do not leave this to chance. There is far too much at stake.

Be a Google ninja. Understand your loans. Understand your options. If you are not going to, then hire the student loan experts who will guide you to the optimal student loan repayments. It is worth it.

So back to the PSLF, if you are 22 years old, and you will have your student loan theoretically repaid in 10 years, then you could probably split a 12% savings rate, prioritized between whatever the payment required for the PSLF is and saving for retirement (hopefully enough to max the match). Those suckers will be paid off in a reasonable time-frame.

Finally, let's say you have a lot of student loans, and because you make a bit more money than the average young person (maybe you're a doc or a lawyer), I recommend slaying that debt aggressively. Live like you don't make much money. Get your savings rate to 20%+, refinance the student loan debt for, say, 5 years, and eat beans and rice to make those payments and to max out the retirement plan. (You need the tax deduction!)

Meet Jane. She went to acupuncture school, a longtime dream of hers, but when she graduated with $90,000 in student loan debt at the same time that she was having her first of three children, she realized it was not going to be as straightforward as she hoped. She and her husband Derrick had a choice to make: move into a bigger house or renovate the one they were in to make room for the kids. The only issue was that they both valued Jane's time with the babies and didn't like the idea of her having to take a full-time acupuncture job during those precious years. Jane had started her own fledgling practice that allowed her to have the flexibility she wanted and needed. It just didn't pay a lot at the beginning.

Student loans scared Jane and stressed her out. She kept deferring them as the budget got tighter after having children. After a lot of discussion, Jane and Derrick made a pivotal choice: Pay off the student loans. Fast. Forget the home purchase or renovation. They could live in any condition if it meant getting out from under those loans.

They made the decision to build a budget for their family living on Derrick's salary alone. Everything Jane made went to the student loans. Sometimes she was barely able to make a payment. Other times she added extra or even doubled it. Extra money and windfalls went to it. Jane said that as they saw the student loan balance go down, the desire for a new home began to wane. But another thing happened that was unexpected. Jane believes the focus on paying off her student loans as a goal for herself and Derrick actually drove her to build her business. She now has a very successful acupuncture business, and, most importantly, informed me in 2019 that she had paid off the last dollar of her student loans. In under 2 years.

I could write an entire book focusing only on how to manage student loans, but for our purposes here, I can tell you this: In every single case of a client who had buried her head in the sand with regard to paying off student loans, it cost her dearly. Face yours. Especially since you might end up better off. By facing them, you could end up with a lower payment and (if you are in public service) have them paid off faster. It sounds too good to be true, but the federal government has many repayment options. Only a few of them offer income-driven re-payments, or paying just a percentage of your income with some form of forgiveness of the remaining balance. Or you choose to slay your loans quickly and refinance them into a lower interest loan to hasten the repayment. Remember that you don't just have your loans to worry about. Before you say "I do" be sure to find out how many loans are on the other side and what the plan is for those loans.

In summary, this is the moment where I dig your head out of the sand and bring you up into the sunlight to face, no, rather to command, your student loans. You must take charge of these. Now. Not tomorrow. Not in three days. Like, pick up the phone this very minute and get a plan in place.

Saving for Retirement When You Get Pay Increases

Remember our compound interest chart before, assuming that Olivia never got pay raises? I did that purposefully to keep the point clear that time and investments can do a lot of the work to grow your savings. Well, what if Olivia did start getting raises? Maybe initially those raises were to keep up with inflation, but then over time she started making more money, say from rising in the ranks at a company. If you think about it, if she kept saving 10% then she could end up without enough retirement, particularly if those pay increases were dramatic. That makes sense because her early years reflected her saving on a smaller salary and planned for a lower lifestyle in retirement. Now she will want to carry her new lifestyle in retirement.

This is an easy fix. Every time Olivia gets a pay raise, she should shuttle part of that pay raise into a higher retirement savings rate, and then she can enjoy the rest. If she gets a 5% raise, maybe 2% gets added to her retirement to get to 12% and then the other 3% adds to her lifestyle.

For some people who were late to the savings game and staring at a 30% savings rate to have a chance to retire on time, maybe you can get to 20% but then use all subsequent pay raises to get to 30%. It's a fine strategy if you are confident those pay raises will come (and that you will actually follow through on the commitment when the time comes). I still believe we need to get to our ideal savings rate immediately, but this is a good plan B if that is just not available.

Never Ever Ever Ever Ever Cash Out

I met a woman who saved 10% her whole life but had very little to show for it. How could that be? She changed jobs frequently, and every time she left, she cashed out of her retirement plan. She told me it was her greatest regret in life and that every time she did it, she didn't understand the magnitude of the opportunity cost of letting that money grow and accumulate.

Never ever ever cash out of your retirement. When you put money into your retirement plan, I want you to consider that money gone, never to be touched again until you are retired. Think about it like this. If you made a car payment for two years, would you ever go back to the dealership and ask for the sum total of those car payments back? Nope. When you write a check for a car payment, that money is gone.

This has to be your mentality with the retirement account. This is not the place to "find money"—ever—not for loans and not for withdrawals. It can seem so tempting, especially in the case of emergencies. But I promise, you need to look elsewhere. In fact, that is why I am so passionate about the next topic: emergency funds. I believe in them wholeheartedly JUST to protect your precious retirement fund. Just to make sure you are never tempted to cash out. In the ship that will sail into the sunset of your retirement, these are the lifeboats strapped to the side of your vessel.

I have had people cash out for moving expenses, health expenses, or even just because it was there and it was a small amount—only $5,000. What's the difference? First of all, cashing out costs you so much. All that hard-earned money you scraped away to save, and now you have to pay income taxes at those top brackets (assuming you have been working all year so you are at the top rate), *and* if you are under 60 you have to pay a 10% penalty to the government on top of that for cashing out early. Every dollar you look at in your account, after cashing out, would look something more like 50 cents.

Just don't do it. Every time you get a new job, the first order of business is to roll your old plan into your new retirement plan. When I talk to people leaving companies that we do retirement plans for, I ask them to take their money with them. Keep rolling it forward. It is absolutely the best decision.

Don't Have a Retirement Plan?

Don't have access to a company retirement plan? Then you don't have to save for retirement! (Just kidding. Wrong!) I hate to say this, but you are going to have to work a lot harder to save for retirement. Some organizations estimate that between 40%–60% of workers don't have access to one. This could be because you work for a company that doesn't offer one or you are in the gig economy. You run errands, drive for Uber, nanny, etc. Hey, you hustle, and you have the flexible schedule that comes with it. But with the freedom of that flexible schedule comes a lot of responsibility with, yes, your finances.

Side point—report your money. Pay your taxes. People are scared of the IRS for a reason. It stinks to pay taxes, but we all gotta do it. And you need to be paying into social security. This is another important retirement source. While we won't know exactly what the social security retirement benefit will look like over time, paying into it is certainly something you want to be doing so that it is available to you. I won't harp on this, but it is part of adulting (and not going to prison).

Back to saving for retirement. Except in cases where you make a lot of money (google "deductible IRA phaseout when you don't have a workplace retirement plan"), you can contribute to either an Individual Retirement Account (IRA) or a Roth Individual Retirement Account (Roth IRA). These suckers work just like the retirement plans we discussed before. The only difference is you have to open them yourself and physically fund them yourself.

If you are in that 18- to 30-year-old range, I just really love the Roth IRA deal. Pay the taxes now, and don't pay them ever again.

Do not be intimidated. People open these all the time. You can pull up the websites at Vanguard, Fidelity, or Schwab to open one, but even better, consider picking up the phone and calling them. This is a great chance to ask questions and learn how they work. Plus, sometimes in the process there is some jargon involved, like, do you want to reinvest dividends? "Oh my gosh! Stop right there. I can't. Not right now," says your brain. Silence! Yes, you can. (And, yes, you want to reinvest the dividends. We will get to the investments in a second.) Do not be sidelined or intimidated by the jargon. Push through. Demand answers and explanations. Don't be afraid to ask the same question again until you understand. Also, when you are talking to those institutions, a really good way to get advice when they can't necessarily give it, is to ask, "What do people typically do?" Most of the time, they can answer that question.

A point of distinction—there are local offices that might have those names on them like Fidelity or Schwab, but that's not what I am suggesting. They have advisors who can set up Roth IRAs using those platforms, but as a starter investor, you are not going to be interesting to these advisors. Also, you don't want to accidentally wander into an advisor's office who also sells insurance. In technical terms, I am recommending that you open a "non-managed account." When you don't have much money in the non-managed account, you have fees just like the big accounts but without the advice that comes with those fees. Think about this, if you put in $6,000, and they charge 1.5% in fees, that is only $90. Trust me, no one in that industry will work hard for $90. Better to avoid the fee, altogether, and just set up your own account and keep that hard-earned $90 in *your* pocket. If you go straight to the websites of the big institutions and request the non-managed account, they are really good about helping you get your account set up. And, while you don't technically have a human assigned to your account, they have people available to answer questions.

Let me not pretend this is always a walk in the park. You have to put in a little elbow grease to get an account open, but I can promise it won't be nearly as hard as you might think.

Your Roth IRA is now opened, but next you have to fund it (i.e. put money in it). The IRS tells you that you are only allowed to add so much. In 2020, for individuals under 50, that maximum is $6,000. You can do the math of how much you want to put in, and if you are under 30, that is 10% of what you make every year.

Just add up the income you make each month, on average, and take 10% of that. Remember, we don't want this to be some hard decision you make every month. Automation is your best friend! For instance, let's say you make $60,000 per year, and you want to save 10% for retirement. That would be $6,000 in savings every year, or $500 per month. Did you know you can auto draft out of your business or personal checking $500 per month directly into your Roth IRA? You can simulate your own retirement account just like you would have in a company retirement plan.

From there, you need to invest it. We will discuss that part in a second, but to me the best investment available for IRAs is a target date retirement fund for the year you plan to retire, most likely at age 65. Just do the math of when you will turn 65, and match that date to the closest target date fund year.

Another quick point: when you don't have a retirement account, you can also consider other things to do if you anticipate one day having an account. You could use these years to pay off student loan and credit card debt aggressively. You could also use early years to build the *second* most important account—your emergency fund.

Start Your Emergency Fund While Saving

You need a pile of cash. Trust me. It is technically called an emergency fund, but it will likely be a source of freedom in your life that you can't even imagine right now. In the past three years, I personally know three people who have left jobs, not because they were terrible or abusive, but because they just weren't right. They all three worried about ending up in a new job that would be more of the same, so they all walked away. They rested. They soul searched. They evaluated what their strengths and drivers were. They thought about how they wanted to spend their years on this earth. And they all, all three of them, ended up in jobs and personal situations they never could have dreamed up. While there is no guarantee that leaving a job without having a job can lead to something better, the power and the ability to walk away is what you are looking for.

I have had clients during our planning relationship who had terrible and unexpected things happen. They were laid off, or they were victims of car accidents or health events. In all of these cases, the events were truly unexpected. The clients who were unprepared found the events not only physically and emotionally, but financially, devastating.

We often assume that tomorrow will be the same because yesterday and the day before were that way. Sometimes I even fall into that trap. While we can't and shouldn't consume ourselves with worry that "the other shoe is about to drop" all the time, we do need to prepare. The only thing that can make personal tragedy worse is to add significant debt into the mix. Finances can be known to cause ill effects on health and even to compound health crises. A lack of savings can be detrimental in these situations.

Ladies, I want something bigger than a cash pile to insulate you against tragedy. I want your cash power to be your source of power. It's a secret knowledge that you walk around with all day long—a comforting reminder that you are taking good care of yourself. You go to sleep knowing it's there. You don't spend it. You only add to it. You always have it. That's the rule. The emergency fund is just like the retirement account. Once that deposit is made, consider it a solemn promise not to spend it.

When *do* you spend it? When it is time to spend it, you will know. The emergency fund is not for tires. It is not for a new roof. It is not for new clothes. It is for emergencies or major opportunities. If you are asking the question whether you should tap into it, then you have answered the question. It's not time.

Funding an emergency fund is hard. Not spending it is even harder. Please heed my best advice, which is similar to my earlier advice if your employer has a waiting period for retirement accounts: Set up a savings account that is not at your regular bank. You do not want this account to tempt you on a daily basis. If you are like me, it is so hard to peacefully coexist with money just sitting there. That cash is a siren call that sometimes whispers, sometimes screams, *Come spend me*! Ugh, especially the emergency fund. It doesn't even have a job. I don't even know why I should have it. But I do know we need a new couch, and there is the perfect one right now on sale! Surely that's a better use?

Stop! It's a trap! An emergency fund is so important, but if you are going to rely on your brain to believe that it is best used as an emergency fund all day every day, you are playing with fire. I promise, I have had a parade of clients who report having an emergency fund that is $200 today, sure, but was actually $5,000 right after they got the bonus and funded it. But then there was the new alternator for the car, the leaking roof, that landscape project, the new washer they desperately needed . . . etc. There is always something to fill in the blank with its pressing need.

Now, if you own a home, you will need money for all those things, and we will get to how to save for them (and a discussion on whether buying a new home makes sense in the first place). If you own a car, you will need money to repair and replace it. If you work in a professional job, you will need money for clothes. All those things need to be considered, planned, and saved for. But you cannot use the emergency fund for these things. Not ever.

Back to safely funding and peacefully coexisting with the first pile of cash you will ever have in your life. (If you have had one and not raided it—fist bump. I am totally impressed. You are rare.) I recommend setting up an online savings account, like through Ally Bank, Synchrony Bank, or American Express. They typically pay a higher interest rate than a local bank, largely because they don't have the overhead of brick and mortar branches. They can pass that benefit on to you as a customer, via a higher interest rate on your savings account. After you open that account, go to your employer and ask them to payroll deduct a small amount from every paycheck into it. Verify that the first deposit went through, and then let the magic take over. Forget about it. Forget you have it. Forget you are funding it. Consider it encased in glass that reads: "Break only in case of emergency."

In an emergency, you will remember, you will break the glass, and that will be a sizable account.

We will talk about savings accounts later in Step 2 of the pay yourself first system, but the reason I tucked it in up here with the retirement account is to insist on its creation. The goal ought to be to have three to six months of spending in the account, and it may take a while to get there. That's okay! You simply cannot fund a retirement plan over time and then essentially "break even" on your finances. Something will go wrong. And when it does, you will look for the closest pile of cash. If that is your retirement account, that is really, really bad. It is always a bad idea to take money out. Even loans are bad. You then have to repay them while you are trying to save, so people often end up stopping their contributions until they pay back the loan over several years. Retirement plans are not ATMs. They are not sources of cash. They are available for your future self who might somehow have to figure out how to live for 30 years without pay. She needs that money. Don't take it away from her.

Tell the World You're a Saver

Save, and please tell the world. We live in a hyper-conspicuous consumption environment. The economy needs you to spend everything you have. Rich people are getting richer because they are saving and investing in companies; if you are buying up all that stuff those companies make, then you are not the one getting richer. Vicki Robin knows what you are up against to become a saver: "[S]aving has clearly become un-American. Even the language of modern economics promotes consumption. What else would we do with 'disposable' income besides dispose of it?"[37]

It's time for a new era of conspicuous saving. **In a world of consumption, not everyone gets to participate equally. But in the world of saving, we can all participate equally.** How? By percentages. If you save 10% in your 20s, you will be able to maintain your lifestyle in retirement. So can your co-worker, your sister, your friend. You want this for yourself and you want this for the people you care about.

One thing I have learned in the past nine years is I *never* know what a financial situation will be when clients walk through the door. They can drive up in a Mercedes and have $10,000 in credit card debt and a large home that has next to no equity in it. Or they can drive up in a 20-year-old Honda and have $1 million in savings. They are stressed, or they are hopeful. I can't know which it is when they walk through the door. Translation: you don't either.

You can't tell that your neighbor is doing well because they have a nice ride. What they are driving also doesn't mean they are *not* doing well. You can't know.

I understand the pressure to look successful. Sometimes we need people to think we are successful to get more success, or at least we tell ourselves that. That has been an argument from clients in legal or medical professions and those trying to build their own businesses. Looking the part with a fancy car, house, or membership to a social club can give the air of success, the thinking being that if people believe you are successful they might be more likely to use your services. Sounds good, but that's not really how it works. Remember, the brain is a tricky thing, and these are the arguments the brain uses to get what it wants. No one is paying attention to you in the same way you are paying attention to you. I can name some very successful people in the generations just above you that I have worked with around the country who drive modest cars and live in modest houses, meanwhile with millions in the bank. Although he could have driven any car in the world, Walmart founder and billionaire Sam Walton famously drove a 1979 truck until his death in 1992.

The flip side is that spending can kill opportunity. Living a life to the edge of your means gives you no room to pursue opportunities.

Interestingly, *because* I have gotten to have this conversation over and over, *because* I know the truth about people's finances, I have a rare advantage over your vantage point. I have learned that none of it matters. Trying to look successful only brings pain. Trying to dress the part is not strategic; it stems from the fear of losing friends, of not fitting in, of not appearing to be what you are trying to emulate. If money and prestige are what you have to put on to fit in, then you are buying into a lifetime of pain.

I have clients and personal friends who make a lot of money and others who are teachers or nonprofit workers and make very little money. They share that they live below their means, whatever those means are. They have friends and are satisfied. They might drive a Jaguar or a clunker, but they are true friends.

What I love is the open conversation about money that I can have with friends, not just clients. Sure, people feel like I hold a safe space to openly discuss money without judgement, but they also foster this safe space in their other relationships well. And when you have a support network of folks who can discuss running out of their dining-out budget and ask about staying in rather than going out, then you will find it much easier to save.

If you are brave enough to have an honest dialogue about your financial goals and desire to save and live below your means, you will positively impact those around you. I find that people of nearly every income, even most who inherit wealth, still must have some version of a budget or spending limitation. My company services many highly paid physicians, and they will be the first to tell you they live within a budget.

Saving and living below our means is a conversation for our generation. Imagine the pain that we can avoid and our friends can avoid if you, I, we can bravely open up a conversation that has been considered inappropriate for generations. It's time that we change that.

INVEST YOUR SAVINGS

"Our investing brains often drive us to do things that make no logical sense—but make perfect emotional sense."　　　　—Jason Zweig[38]

There is no easy way to do this, but I just have to break it to you: You gotta invest. It may just look a little different than you're expecting.

There is no difference in gender better highlighted than in the investing step. Many men seem to live for the day to invest. The thrill and the conquest are just too sweet to resist. They save money just for the investing part—not necessarily for the "can I retire" or "can I send my kids to college" parts.

Picture it. The moment they strut into the arena. They are the matador, and the market is the bull. They will win. They have secrets no one else has, secrets that will bring the market to its knees, similar to how the Picadors weaken the bull before the kill. Spoiler alert: It doesn't work this way. There really aren't any big secrets.

My children and I love reading the book *Ferdinand*. It's the perfect parallel. I won't pretend to speak for all women, but in my experience and in general, women walk into the arena, look at the crowds, forgive the bull, and take him back home where they will live with him in peace and harmony. We want no part of the kill. We really don't care about beating the market. We don't see the point of trying to win (and it's not really winning, anyway, as you'll see). We just want our money to grow.

Women have been led to believe that we are missing something—the killer instinct—and that it is the only approach that works. I am telling you right now that your desire to *not win* is a winning strategy. Yep, you can open the other eye now. This is not going to be as terrible as you might think. Remember how women, in wide measures from stock picking to investing their money, end up with superior returns? It's because the matador actually loses to the bull more than the public believes. Ninety percent of the time, in fact, over the long haul. So, women are calling a truce with the market. Just joining it rather than beating it means we perform average, and average in an environment where the majority of the players are trying to win means "winning" (if we really need to use that term).

I know that argument's not good enough. Here's why we invest. We need all the help we can get to achieve this retirement thing. Remember the charts a while back, demonstrating the difference in saving when we start in our 20s versus in our 30s? They assume a little over 5% rate of return. It would end up being just enough to be able to retire in our 60s. But what if, instead of investing money in the stock and bond market with an expectation to grow our money at 5%+, we put it in a simple savings account that grows at 2%. What would we have to do? We would have to save *double* to likely end up in the same place.

Let's walk hand in hand through this. By the time we are done, I predict you will be equipped with the knowledge and confidence to do this investing thing. Many women (and men) don't want to invest because they don't understand how it fits into a plan and why the risk is worth taking. Investing is not gambling. In gambling, the house always wins. While there can be elements of gambling in the relative choices people make with investing, they are not typically the same as going to Vegas. Most importantly, although it involves some guessing, the investing that you will be doing will look little like gambling.

You are not in a game where someone wins and another loses. You are in a fight for your future, a fight for your money, a fight to live life on your own terms. Investing is a tool in that fight—not an enemy like in the matador/bull scenario. Investing is here to help you.

Some people use the mystery of the stock market as a reason to not *save* at all. That's an interesting approach when you follow the logic. "The whole investing thing makes me nervous. I just can't do it. Instead, I am going to do what I know and live in the now. At least I know where my money is going."

This is a massive justification to let the brain run amuck with your finances, because it is the argument to keep spending. What, I ask, is the return on a dollar spent on that fabulous shirt that was on sale, that shirt that would be "capsule," or even better—my absolute favorite thing I have ever heard: "investment jeans." What in the heck? No! There is NO such thing as investment jeans. Jeans are not an investment. You had money. You went to the store and bought jeans. Then you didn't have money. Yes, you wore the jeans. Yes, you looked fantastic. But unless someone paid you to model those fabulous-looking jeans, then they are not investment jeans.

When you invest money, you are wanting to take a pile of money and grow it over a long period of time. And you will get rewarded in your investment by taking on risk, or, in other words, by being comfortable with the fact that sometimes your money will take a breather along the way because of that risk.

So, let's get started.

Bucking the Intimidation of Jargon

You will likely have two types of investments in your portfolio (fancy, right?), and they are stocks and bonds. (There are other types of investments out there like real estate, annuities, insurance, etc. Please don't go there. Feel free to read various blogs and listen to multiple podcasts on the issue, but they are rarely a good deal. Plus, you are not likely to run up against them in your retirement plan at work, which is where the majority of people will—and should—build their nest eggs.)

Stocks

> 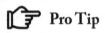 **Pro Tip**
>
> If prompted, always choose the option to re-invest dividends. When those earnings are paid, you can either pocket the cash or have them rein-vested to buy new shares of stock. The latter is how you get rich, so always remember to reinvest. It happens automatically after you check that box.

A stock is a piece of a company. When you purchase one, you agree to become an owner in a company, and as the owner, expect to get paid by the company's stock growing in value. In other words, you bought it at $10, and it grew to $15. You made $5 in profit. Some stocks will allow you to make additional money via payouts to the owners (that's you!) of what the company earned every quarter. These are called dividends to the owner.

Stocks inherently have risk. It's the risk you are getting paid for when you buy stocks. Stocks go up and down all day long, week after week. Historically, they have gone up a lot more than they've gone down, and that's the expectation you will have when you buy them.

The stock market is where shares of stocks are traded. You can pick a company from which you consume a lot like Facebook, Walmart, or Apple, to name a few, and go buy a piece of them. I do not recommend this. The practice of buying individual stocks, which I earlier referred to as the "loser's game," is one where we think we have more insight than the entire market. What I can tell you is that the stock market is smarter than you, than me, than everyone. We can't beat it. I promise I will prove it to you in a bit. We just have some jargon to get through first.

The point is that these companies are publicly traded. You and I are the public, and we can go and buy them while the market is open. (Other companies are private, so unless you are a family member, executive, or there is some other exception, pieces of those companies are not available for purchase.)

When we hear on the radio or read from a news source that "the market" is up or down, what is happening is that different companies measuring certain collections of stocks are reporting how that collection is doing. The most popular measure that many people recognize is "the Dow" or the Dow Jones Industrial Average, which basically measures a very small collection of the largest companies in the market. The S&P 500 is lesser used but a better proxy of how "the market" is doing. It measures the performance of 500 of some of the largest companies in the U.S.

We call these measures "indexes" because we just need more useless jargon out there. Actually, you need to commit this particular one to memory. It's gonna come up later, and I need you to know it. Go into the deep recesses of your brain that understand the common word "average" and replace it with "index." We are looking at, on average, how the top 500 U.S. companies are doing. Are they up or down (on average)? By how much? But we fancy schmancy people need you to think it's a lot more complicated, so over a vodka martini we chortle over the latest "move" in the S&P (short for S&P 500 *index* which is just the fancy word for average). Got it?

To be clear, when I talk about "the market" being up or down, I am saying that some collection of stocks representing the market is a good proxy for what you are experiencing if you are in the stock market, especially if you are in the stock market in the way I want you to be in the stock market. (We'll get to it later. I don't want to spoil the surprise yet.)

One more thing: No two stocks are alike. Some stocks you will buy are part of big companies and some are part of small companies. Easy, right? Hold my beer.

A large company in the stock market is called, wait for it, a "large cap" stock. This is shorthand for large capitalization, meaning there is a large amount of "capital"ization. Capital is a fancy word for money. So think "large 'money'ization," or "lots of money." Do you see what is happening here? When someone talks about investing in "large cap stocks," they are using language that is made up, shorthand speak for other industry insiders. The other way to say it is, "We buy big companies in our portfolio." Aaaaaaaand breathe.

By the same logic, we have "mid cap" and "small cap" stocks, or shares of mid-sized companies and small-sized companies.

Large companies (large cap stocks) are not expected to grow very fast, but we like them for their dividends. They are so mature and so efficient that they tend to make a lot of money. Since they don't expect to grow a lot, they don't need that extra money to invest in their own growth. So, they pay us as owners. Now, large companies can and do grow. Look at Apple, Google, and Facebook. They just keep growing. But most of the time, we shareholders just expect the big companies (large caps) to grow steadily and pay us dividends (uh capital, uh profits, uh money). Yep, pay us money. On a quarterly basis.

The mid- and small-cap stocks are expected to be zoomier. They hold on to cash profits to put back into the company so they can zoom some more. Some of the companies don't even make cash. They *lose* money! But they are expected to grow so fast that investors are cool with that. An example of that is Uber. It lost, wait for it, $5 BILLION in one quarter alone, in 2019. Why would we buy it? Well, you probably have it installed on your phone. And the expectation is that over time with enough people using it, Uber will eventually make a lot of money.

Which it might do. Or it might not do. Or it will get replaced by another company that might do it better. And if it allows itself to get traded publicly (to "go public"), then you would own it, too.

We just can't know what these stocks will do. Which is why we

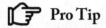

Pro Tip

Do not buy individual stocks (companies). Ever. We will get to how to buy stocks in a second. Just wanted to keep making this very clear.

set expectations in our brains. Always assume when you are buying a stock that five years later, it will be worth less than what you bought it for. Yep, you heard me right. I want you to expect that your money, all that hard-earned savings that you have socked away, will be worth less in these first few years after you put it into the market. More importantly, that is really okay.

How many people have started their savings careers right before a drop in the market? You might say, well, just wait for stocks to go down and then buy before they go up. Sounds simple, but that is market timing. And market timing has brought the strongest matadors to their knees. We can never know when it will go up or down—just like that Vanguard tool I introduced you to earlier, it's a guessing game because we don't have a crystal ball. One of my favorite sayings from John C. ("Jack") Bogle, founder of Vanguard, on what to do during market volatility, is "Don't do something. Just stand there."[39]

We do know that based on history and our expectations for a continuously improving U.S. economy that over the *long-run*, stocks will go up. Over the *short-run*, if you assume they will go down, then you can more easily mentally stick with the plan. In other words, if you tell your brain that you expect your money to go down, and then it does, you will be less likely to reverse course and get out of the stock market before it improves once more. The stock market going down from time to time is a very big problem. People go into the stock market not realizing that they are getting paid to take on risk, and then at the slightest move downward they bail. But that's not you. You will look at the numbers and realize that your money going down is a round trip ticket with going up on the other end. My best suggestion is after you put it in there, don't look, because it will keep your emotions from riding the (sometimes a little too scary) super roller coaster.

Also, this is important, do not expect to take your money out. If you have even the slightest inkling that you would have to take money out within five years, then it has no business being in the stock market.

When I say "put your money in" or "take your money out," I am being vague on purpose. We are going to discuss later what investing looks like on a practical level. Chances are, you may have already done just this and not realized it through your company retirement plan. A couple months ago, a woman approached me and said she wanted to invest in stocks and bonds and worried she was late to the game. I asked her to tell me a little about how she saved, assuming she was going to tell me that all her money was in a savings account. To my surprise, she said she had her money in her company retirement account. We pulled it up, and when I took a look I understood how she was confused. She was invested in stocks and bonds, but nowhere did her investments say "stocks" or "bonds." I explained how she was invested in funds that buy and sell stocks and bonds for her. I could see a sigh of relief when she realized that she was not on the sidelines but very much in the game of growing her money.

It is very easy to get into the stock market, so don't worry about that part. I just want you to understand that once you are in, I don't want you getting cold feet. When the world realized that the COVID-19 epidemic was becoming a pandemic, the expectations for the global economy turned bleak. Fast. Before we could even figure out how to wear face masks, investors saw the value of their stocks drop nearly 35%, temporarily erasing years of gains in their portfolios. Some people, frightened and shaken to the core, got out during that drop, unable to handle the loss and worried they could lose even more. They figured that it was better to lock in those losses and wait to get back in. But it doesn't work that way. The stock market rebounded. It could go back down again. Or it could keep going up. We can't know either way—we just have to stay in it, knowing that we're committed for the long haul.

Bonds

A bond is different from a stock; it is a loan to a company or a government. You expect to get paid back, and most of the time you expect a bond to pay you interest on your money in the meantime. There's not a lot to say about bonds. Think of stocks as your favorite Uncle Alden who plays Legos for hours on the floor, surprises everyone Christmas day with lavish gifts, but on rare occasions doesn't show up at the last minute, unleashing waves of disappointment. On the other hand, bonds are your steady grandma. Enough said.

We like bonds for their stability and income. We like getting paid cash. Especially in retirement. Some people call bonds "fixed income" just because of the interest payments. You know you will get paid.

Bonds are not without risk. There are risky bonds out there that don't pay off. And those in danger of not being able to pay back the loan have higher interest.

Also, bonds can go up or down in value. If I have a bond that pays 5% interest a year, but the new bonds that just came out are paying only 3% per year, then you would rather have my 5% bond, right? If I paid $1,000 for my bond, you will pay me more than $1,000 for it now. In a rising interest environment, the price of the old bonds will go down. In a falling interest environment, the price of the old bonds will go up. There's a lot more we could discuss on bonds. Feel free to google "how bonds work" if this is riveting to you, but I need to stop here. I will lose you dear folks, and we haven't even gotten to mutual funds yet. I need you to stick with me, so grab some caffeine if you need to.

Mutual Funds

You could go out there into the stock market and start picking and choosing, buying up individual stocks and bonds to go into your portfolio. Or you could more appropriately stick to your day job and let someone else buy those stocks and bonds for you, and your neighbor, and your friend, and thousands of people you have never met.

Instead of buying shares of stocks or bonds (or both), you can buy into mutual funds which purchase stocks and/or bonds on your behalf, and there are thousands of these out there with trillions of dollars in them.

Mutual funds are a great way to invest, and if you have a company retirement plan, they are probably the only options you have, anyway.

But let me warn you, looking at this list of investments could cause ill health effects. Yep, a tightening in the chest, warning signals in the brain. Danger ahead. Regret behind. See, the problem with this "list of mutual funds" that are doing something so simple, so practical, and so convenient for us is that they are named in nonsensical ways and are nearly impossible for the average person to sort out.

Each mutual fund takes on a "style" of investing, meaning it wants to only buy stocks/bonds with a certain flavor. For instance, maybe it only buys big companies that are better than what investors believe they are (translation, they are on sale cuz people don't want to buy 'em). The idea is that they are "undervalued," or thought to be selling at less than they actually are worth. So, portfolio managers create a fund of just those companies, but instead of naming this fund "Undervalued Big Companies Fund," they name it the "Gutierrez Large Cap Value Fund." Go grab your paper bag and start taking long, easy breaths. Put your head between your knees. I promise not to throw any more of those out there.

Let's simulate this moment. You are in HR signing up to save, *the most important thing you will do in life*. You make this great choice to scrape 10% of everything you make out of your check, and you are feelin' good. But then this list of funds pops up in front of you, and you start to panic. You find yourself going through the list of all the things you *should have* done to prepare you for this moment. What if you had taken that finance class? Did you sleep through the math class where they discussed large versus small cap and growth versus value stocks?

(Rest easy: They don't teach large cap, small cap, any cap in standard high school or college courses. You missed nothing.)

I took the finance classes, but it wasn't until I was on the inside, doing the actual work of analyzing stocks that I knew what it was all about. In other words, this is not about you and what you don't know, so turn your finger away from your own face and point it in another direction.

Buying a house is a huge deal. When you buy one, there is a stack of jargon-heavy papers that are put in front of you at the "closing," or the moment you take possession of the house. During the closing a patient title company representative goes page by page, paper by paper, explains what it means, sits quietly while you read, and then directs you where to sign. Imagine if you had to just walk into that room and sort through all those things and start signing? Wouldn't you be overwhelmed?

Saving for retirement is a bigger deal than buying a house. It is the moment when you are making the most important decision of your life. But here is a baffling menu of investments and no one is there to help or explain. HR can't help you because the liability is too big for them to help you pick a fund.

You are sitting there, alone with the list. You might think, as many do, "Let's do this later." But don't do this later. Don't put this off. You won't pick it back up.

If this stuff is literally freaking you out, then please do not worry. I want you to grow a couple of inches taller, understand that no part of this makes inherent sense, stop feeling responsible for knowing what any of that jargon means, and ask HR for the phone number of the advisor. This is the advisor's job. They picked the line-up. They can help you pick out which ones to put in your plan and at what percentages. It's going to take a minute, and some deep breaths, but remind yourself that you are doing the leg work now so you don't have to worry about it again. Also remember, **it is worth it to put in the time that it might**

BUT FIRST, SAVE 10

take to watch a movie or spend an evening out on the town to understand how to make the most important decision of your life.

If this stuff seems interesting, albeit foreign, then immerse yourself into this world. Turns out the complication is much ado about nothing. All those big words are part of an industry that is in serious peril. They are part of an industry being replaced by robots, like nearly every other industry out there. They just don't realize it yet. But it's good for you to know that intellectually.

If this stuff doesn't seem interesting, know that you will in the end probably do just as well. People who take on complicated, time consuming investing strategies statistically cause themselves to do worse with their money. Remember that chart I showed you before on incremental effort toward picking investments? Incremental effort, or extra homework, on investments will not make you top of this class.

Passive Index Funds

⋮ "Don't look for the needle—buy the haystack." —Jack Bogle[40]

A couple years ago, I joined a large endowment and was the first female trustee. We had one job which was to oversee the investments and approve withdrawals for the use of the endowment. At the time, there were three money managers investing the fund. The first thing I asked when I joined the board was simple: "How are the investments doing?" We seemed to be doing well but it was unclear by how much. So I requested that the board put it to the test.

We hired a professor at a local university to run a simple, independent analysis. He took the dollars we started with and then simulated the investments in index funds. (We will get to that.) In other words, he put the money in the indexes, themselves, that were the benchmarks for performance. Over this nearly 15-year period, the difference in how much money we would have had in the simulated index funds versus what we actually had in our account was several million dollars more. It was enough of a difference that the board decided to simplify our portfolio and self-manage it. We realized that we were paying a few hundred thousand dollars in fees to the money managers every year, only to end up doing worse than the market average. And by switching to average performance in the market we could reduce our fee from several hundred thousand to $30,000. By reducing our fees, we are likely to end up with *more* money in the end, *more* money to give to those who the money was helping.

I remember when the idea was initially proposed, the board was uncertain. But our board chair was rather entrepreneurial and took the time to figure it out. Importantly, he was not in the investments industry. Once he took the time to figure out our strategy and understand what would be required of the board to rebalance the investments quarterly and request withdrawals, he realized it was more straightforward than the board thought. The board agreed, and every quarter we meet and agree to the calculation from our board chair. He carries out the rebalancing. He gets approvals to request the checks to fund our benefiting organization. The check gets sent for the charitable operations. It's that simple.

In 1975, a man named John C. "Jack" Bogle created something called an index fund. He did it out of acknowledgement of what was happening in the market—all those mutual funds were not doing what they said they would do. They were not "beating the market." And the analysis was really skewed in favor of mutual funds. He couldn't even measure the funds that did so poorly that investors pulled their money out, and the funds went away. So, he was looking just at the mutual funds still around.

Now, the people picking stocks and bonds in these mutual funds are smart people. I have met many of them. But their Achilles heel is one thing alone: their fees. They simply cannot beat the market on a sustained basis and beat their own fee. The fee on a mutual fund is called an "expense ratio" (more jargon—ugh), and a typical expense ratio for a managed mutual fund is between .5% and 1%.

No big thang, right? What a small amount. Just a tiny little it-ty-bitty percentage. And, in fact, they make it so easy for you. You don't even have to Venmo or PayPal that fee. Nope, the mutual fund manager just dips his hand into the big pot o' money and takes out his fee. You never even have to find out, much less think about it. The fee is very prominently disclosed, of course, in six-point font under the heading, below the very "clear" fee name called "expense ratio." (Please note my sarcasm.)

Let's say you make $60,000 per year and have saved 10% since your 20s, and by the time you are 50, have about $400,000 in your retirement account. Your average expense ratio is 0.75%. Again, not even a percent! What a small amount.

It's "only" $3,000.

Ok, let's practice this for a second. Go find this thing called a checkbook, if you have one, and write out a check for $3,000 to anyone, for anything.

How does that feel? Good? Bad? Probably the latter. That is a LOT of money, right? It hurts, doesn't it? And guess what? You usually aren't writing a check and so are hardly aware of this fee. It quietly, easily, without you having to work at it, plan for it, panic about it, or even consider it, just disappears from your money to the mutual fund's checking account. From your vacation in retirement to his vacation in retirement. From your ability to write a check for your medical expenses, from your desire to stay in your family home so that the grandkids can come stay with you, from your interest in small luxuries like manicures and upgrading appliances in your own house . . . to the money manager's account.

Here's the absolute craziest part of all: You're gonna need that check book again because he's going to take it out again next year. Gulp.

Remember Jack Bogle? This is what he was seeing. He asked the question: Can we do this better? Can we do this cheaper? And the answer was obvious—if you can't beat the market, join it. If you are just joining the market, then all the expensive managers, support staff, fancy art, Wall Street rent . . . can be paid by someone else. You can simply get in a fund that quietly, inexpensively just buys the whole thing. The whole market. All the stocks. Doesn't try to pick winners. Just picks 'em all. If the stock market is up 3% that year, you are up 3%. These are called index funds, and the strategy of just buying the whole market and not trying to "beat" it is called passive investing.

Ladies, this is for us. This truly is what we have been waiting for. We don't care about beating the market. Most of us have never been interested in the game of trying to kill the bull. Don't you see? We get to strip that element out, simplify a ton, and then float into the retirement sunset. We don't have to stay on top of the best mutual fund manager lists published every year or hire expensive financial advisors who charge their own 1% to then go pick a fund that charges 0.75%, taking our money even further behind. Did you catch this? For real, I am not kidding. It is normal and completely acceptable that you would be paying 1.75%, or $7,000 a year on that same $400,000 life savings. Out of your money.

Nope, we get to push all of that to the side. We get to keep it simple. And simple wins. Every. Single. Time. Watch this.

How much cheaper is passive investing, you ask? Well, back to our $400,000 life savings scenario. Let's say you can buy what you need with passive Vanguard index funds (the funds that Jack Bogle created), and the aggregate cost is 9 basis points (0.09%). That entire cost to you is a whopping $360. Total. Compared to $3,000 assuming you were self-managing your money and buying actively managed mutual funds. Compared to the $7,000 assuming you had hired an advisor to invest your money in actively managed mutual funds.

One final thing is that the old way of picking funds not only required you to care about individual fund performance, but it also made you care about timing the market. You had to care about which types of companies (big or small, value or growth) would do better in the next five years and try to get more of those in your portfolio. Turns out that is a fool's errand. No one can predict it. Again, you are better off not even messing with it.

You are better off buying the whole thing and not looking at it. Not touching it. And waking up one day, ready to retire. And the technology that has truly made it possible for you to dump money into the market and walk away (safely) is the briefly aforementioned target date fund, the single greatest invention for the average investor in the history of the market.

Use Target Date Retirement Funds

You get the idea of how you could invest that might resonate deeply. But how do you physically buy the index funds? What if I told you that you could buy everything you needed in one single fund?

The target date retirement fund is a fund that buys the funds you need on your behalf. It asks everyone within 5 years of retiring at 65 to put their money in sort of a fund stew, if you will, to be invested with the money of others, together for life. Same for folks within 10 years, 15 years, etc. You simply identify the date closest to when you turn 65 and put all your money in that fund. Then the fund, itself, will buy a mix of stocks and bonds appropriate to people targeted to turn 65 within a 5-year range of a year in the future (i.e. 2050, 2055, 2060, 2065).

Olivia is 23 and turns 65 in 2062, so she would choose a target date fund dated 2060, most likely.

The target date retirement fund means you don't have to worry about picking funds, investing in them, rebalancing them, or even thinking about them. You put it in one fund, and it automatically takes you from roughly 90% stocks and 10% bonds in your 20s to about half and half at retirement. From there, it continues to make the account less risky (with less of a percentage of the retirement account in stocks and more in bonds).

I cannot believe what a beautiful thing these are. Some of the smartest people on the planet have made large, aggregate decisions on how the typical person ought to be invested at different points in their lives, and then we all get to benefit from some of the smartest science.

There are great target date funds that are simple with low fees and are offered by companies like Vanguard, Schwab, State Street, Blackrock, and others. These are becoming pretty standard in retirement plans, in fact, and I hope that by the time you are reading this that you will have one as an option.

Recap: How to Invest

If you have a retirement plan at work, fingers crossed that you have a target date fund available to you. Many plans will even default you into your target date fund if you decide not to choose an investment fund.

I assume you are the overachieving type, and your experience is that more work yields better results. Therefore, the target date fund feels like the easy way out, the lazy way that will mean your money does worse.

It's crazy, but simpler wins. Easier wins. Automated wins. Diversification wins.

Market timing loses. Active management loses. Performance chasing loses.

Target date funds are not the lazy choice. They are the best choice. And they allow you to focus on the *most important* decision. What's that? How much to save, of course. Target date funds allow us to completely rejigger the finite amount of time we are going to spend on the topic of personal finance, and we get to go back to evaluating if we are saving enough. If we are paying down debt fast enough. If we are preparing for emergencies enough. If we are putting enough money away for our kids' colleges.

Choose 10%.

Put that 10% into a target date fund.

Set it. And forget it.

If you don't have a retirement plan at work, I highly recommend opening your own retirement account—like a Roth IRA at Vanguard, Schwab, or Fidelity—automating your contributions every month, and investing in the target date funds. It is more work than the convenience of a one-time sign-up at a company, but it is still pretty simple. I have personally walked through the process with lots of young people and am surprised at how intuitive companies make it and how great the customer service folks are at walking people through it when they get confused.

You can do this. I believe in you.

Start Your Emergency Fund

Focus on your retirement plan. Get it going. Set it and forget it.

Then, right away, six months or a year later, or when you get your raise, it's time to start building a large pile of cash. It's a pile, although you don't yet know what you will use it for.

The hard way to build a pile of cash is to open a savings account alongside your main checking account. Remember, like we discussed before? The one you barely can fund and will rob two months later?

Again, the easy way to build a pile of cash is to open a savings account at a bank you don't use. Often, larger companies will have their own credit union available to employees or have a partnership with a credit union. Open one of those accounts and choose some amount that makes sense. Maybe it's just $25. Or $50. Or $100+. Give the account number to payroll and ask them to send that savings every pay period to the bank or credit union.

And then forget about it. *Thank you.* (That is your future self responding—the version of you that is one day going to be grateful you were able to weather a pandemic, start a business, leave a bad job, take a medical leave without financial stress, extend your maternity leave, or whatever it is that you can't foresee now but will be eternally grateful you have it for down the line.)

STEP 2:
PAY FOR FUTURE EXPENSES

Now it's time to boldly step into the life-enhancing world of cash flow management, or being a boss of the rest of your paycheck. Putting money away into distant accounts for retirement and emergency funds benefits from automation but can still be a tough concept for folks like me who love to live in the now. Thanks for hanging in there, even if you're not inspired by compound interest and think you will never leave a job or have an emergency.

The next phase is life enhancing in the now. We are going to discuss opening a series of savings accounts that will fund important things in your life that happen in "lumpy," one-time, or sporadic time intervals. The *old* way of paying for them was to scramble up other money, ultimately resulting in some kind of debt that you would have to labor away to pay back later.

The *new* way of operating is to save ahead of those lumpy expenses. If you ever want to feel powerful with money, this is your time. Need new tires? Money's there. Need to book that vacation with college friends? Money's there. Imagine how that will feel. It is even more exhilarating than you might imagine.

Before we begin, let's take a small step back. The truth is that you could stop at Step 1: Fund your retirement, invest it, and then fund an emergency fund. Then your whole goal in life would be to not go into credit card debt. Lots of people do this successfully. I meet these people all the time who have paid themselves first and successfully managed short-term debt. An expense comes up, they borrow, and then they pay back with interest the subsequent months, sometimes years. It ain't particularly fun, but the important thing is that their retirement savings is cooking in the background. They will probably be okay.

Why not stop at Step 1? Because Steps 2, 3, and 4 will take your money to the next level. Can you imagine a life in which you don't have to worry about huge expenses hitting? (Think about a major medical issue or replacing a whole roof on your house—very expensive!) Imagine a life where you take vacations saved for ahead of time and thus enjoy them more. Imagine a life where you and your partner never have to "fight" about money and if you're single you don't have to wrestle with yourself about it.

As I mentioned earlier, I learned about this cash management system at a financial planning conference in 2014. It is called the First Step Cash Management System™ developed by Marty Kurtz, a pioneer in financial planning and personal finance. He worked mostly with high-net-worth individuals in his practice, and he found that, although you may not think it, almost all clients needed some way to control their cash flow. People making half a million and up per year probably wouldn't want to enter receipts into an app every night (really, neither would anyone else) and would find enveloping cash too cumbersome. So, he developed a system that used bank accounts and auto transfers that would create a fool-proof mechanism to proactively keep people in an overall budget that they had set up using their own priorities.

It was ingenious. People who made a lot of money found a simple way to stay within the very clear confines they had chosen. This ensured that they wouldn't suffer from the creep of spending too much.

Of course, as income rose, luxury could also rise, but it was within the client's planning and control on the front end.

When I heard the presentation, it clicked with me. This was a system that could probably work as well for people who didn't make a lot of money. I immediately started using it to test the system. At that time, I was personally using an intricate Excel spreadsheet that I had created and been using for years. But two months in, using the parallel cash management systems, my Excel spreadsheet was history. What I realized was that while physically entering my spending data could tell me that I occasionally overspent on food, clothes, or babysitters, it was always backward looking. All I could do at that point was pass judgment on my past financial decisions and blame myself, hoping that the shame I felt would keep me in line for the upcoming month. Sometimes it worked, but I didn't like the way all the shame felt. Do you like the way shame feels? I doubt it.

But this new system? It isn't shame- or blame-based: This cash flow system looks forward. Instead of tracking spending in the hopes that there might be something to save at the end of the month, this is a "pay yourself first" system. You fund your retirement, dream savings, and defensive savings (car, rent, home, roof, etc.) first. Next, you make sure you have enough money to pay all your regular monthly bills for the month. Then you spend the rest. I repeat: SPEND THE REST. You get to spend the rest of the money down to zero each month. Feel free to blow it, as a matter of fact. Party time!

All joking aside, this is how generations before us successfully budgeted. While they didn't have the luxury of auto bank transfers, people got paid every week and simply took their cash and funded their bank with savings first, set aside some for the bills they knew they'd have to pay, and then spent the rest. If they knew Johnny would need shoes, they put a little aside each paycheck until there was enough to buy them. The reason previous generations did it this way was simple: They had no other choices; there were no credit cards. When great-grandma looked in her wallet and saw $10, that was all there was. Her wallet did not contain two Visas, a Mastercard, and an American Express. She could not live beyond her means. That is not to say that credit did not exist. But it existed for the purchase of big-ticket items only—houses, cars, business loans, equipment, etc. It did not exist for lunch or shoes, no matter how badly lunch or shoes were needed or wanted.

There are a lot of budgeting systems and apps out there, and they all work for someone. But they don't tend to work for the long-run. This is your forever system that works for the long-term, at any and every income level. It is worth noting that my support of this system is authentic and non-conflicted. Mr. Kurtz and I met briefly during a conference, and I have interviewed him since then for this book. I receive no remuneration from him.

There is nothing hard or complicated about this system, but it is a lot to balance in your mind. I find that teaching it to clients over and over is the best way for them to get the hang of it. For this reason, I will use a lot of repetition throughout the teaching of the system.

Recall that in Step 1, you pay yourself first by funding your retirement. For most people, this will mean contributing directly to your 401(k) pre-tax, or before withholding taxes come out. Once you get your net (take-home) pay, you move to the next step. Step 2: Establish a variety of savings accounts ("squirrel accounts") into which certain pre-determined amounts of money will be automatically transferred. These accounts might have names like, "travel fund," "new car fund," "home repair fund," "529 college fund for the kids," and any other account that is particularly meaningful to you and your life. Step 3: Reduce and then auto-pay your bills. Step 4: Spend the rest. Step 4 has such a beautiful ring to it, right!?

If you haven't done it yet, you can download our worksheet at ButFirstSave10.com and enter your own numbers as we go. This process is iterative, meaning you might find yourself going back and forth through the steps to make your numbers work. A word from experience, you might want to use a pencil. Many people find they have aspirations for Steps 1 and 2, but the realities of Steps 3 and 4 make it difficult to fully fund those earlier and important steps. There might be a tug and pull as you wrestle and negotiate your numbers—cutting a subscription here to add more vacation money there, getting real about your expensive gym membership here to pay more to student loans there—to find the perfect balance.

Some of you might find that you put your numbers in and have more than enough. *This is rare* but a sign of you already having a successful budgeting process in your life or being a natural saver. If you do find there is more money than you need in Step 4, then you might first look to Steps 1 and 2 for that surplus. For instance, adding to Step 1 means you are pulling forward your work optional date. Adding to Step 2 could mean adding to a home down payment fund, college fund, or car fund. I typically don't recommend adding to Step 3 which are bills and payments. Or, if you have all your long-term and intermediate-term goals fully funded, then *enjoy* your money now. That surplus becomes spendable.

Dream Saving is Inspiring

Let me wax poetic for a second about Step 2.

Setting up Step 2 means becoming a dream saver. Dream savers get to take vacations, start companies, change careers, and take sabbaticals. Dream savers have enough saved for their kids to go to college without student loans or with reduced loans. But it's not magic. It's not an event. It's a process. I want each of you who reads this book to become a dream saver, and the process to get there is clear. After you pay your retirement self, you will then set up a series of savings accounts designed to shelter you from unforeseen events, let you travel, and allow you to dream.

I have seen a lot of savings programs that lead with the same concept. Define your dreams and save for them. Then you dump a lot of money each month into a single savings account for all these dreams. The only issue is that in the commingling of dreams, emergency funds, and short-term repair reserves, there is just enough noise for the most common disruption in budgeting—as they used to say, "robbing Peter to pay Paul." We have all done it. We become skilled masters in the art of deceiving ourselves. We are a little short this month after taking that trip to a friend's destination wedding, but we have a lot of money in our savings account. We pull it from there with promises to pay it back. Only, we inadvertently pulled from the part of that savings account that was accumulating money for the big annual car insurance bill because we sort of forgot about it. As a result, the savings account waxes but mostly wanes throughout the year. I bet 90% of you reading this book are nodding your heads. We all do this.

Consider a slightly different approach. Open a savings account with the name of your dream or savings goal on it. Figure out how much to save in a year to achieve it, and then fund the same amount every month. For instance, let's say you dream of taking a large vacation every year that will cost $1,000. To figure out how much you'll need, take $1,000 and divide it by 12: $83.33. Have that amount auto-debited every month from your main checking account and deposited into your savings account titled "vacation."

As a young person right out of college, you would probably just have two to three accounts. But as life gets complicated with marriage, kids, and home buying, it can make sense to add a lot more. This system will just grow alongside your life changes. My husband and I personally have eight savings accounts, seven at a bank, including emergency, health, home repair, car repair and savings, clothing, gifts, and travel. Our 8th is a college savings account via a 529 plan for our kids. But there are so many more options to save for lumpy expenses.

Chances are if you are reading this and in your early 20s, you don't understand the glee that I and many other women my age feel when I describe this piece of the system. We have lived through the large expenses that come up inevitably and experienced the anguish when there is no money to pay for them. This could be Christmas, an air conditioner that suddenly stopped working and cost $500 to fix, or a girls' weekend trip that turned into a shopping trip. When there is no money, we put it on the credit card. As a friend recently articulated, in the months that follow, you are sending your money *backward* to pay that credit card, not *forward*.

When you send money backward, you pay dearly for it because you have used other people's money. When you send money forward, you get paid for it, via interest in a savings account.

Unless you can say, if I don't have any money I won't take a vacation; if I don't have any money I will not fix the air conditioner; if I don't have any money I will not go shopping; if I don't have any money I will not buy anything AT ALL at holiday time, then you absolutely must save ahead for these things.

What about life dreams? My life fundamentally changed because I had a pile of cash and realized I could live quite a while on that pile of cash while I got a business going. Maybe you, too, hope to one day own a business. Open an account called "new business," and fund it each month. You will need capital to start a business and/or money to walk away from your job to make the transition, or more likely, both. The important point is that you must fund these things before you start to spend on them.

I recently sat down with a couple in a retirement plan. He had just gotten a nice salary increase, and she was making a small amount at the same company. They were planning to have a baby in the next two years, and she shared with me her dream to be a stay-at-home mom in their children's younger years. I told them they instantly, that afternoon, should put half of her pay into a retirement account and then whatever money came in from her paycheck, transfer dollar for dollar into a walk-away savings account.

My husband and I have benefited from living on one paycheck or another and banking the rest. If you are newly married and have big plans for someone to be a stay-at-home parent or to start a business, this is a very clever tool for financial independence.

The most common approach is to see how much money is left at the end of the month, sweep it into savings, and call it good. The only problem with this method is that it does not work. And it will likely be obvious to every reader who has stuck with me throughout these pages why: Most of us spend whatever we have. Period. If a few clever dollars manage to elude us and we see them sitting in the account as the month draws to a close, do we burst into song and stuff the dollars in the savings account? No, indeed we do not. We spend those last little stragglers as fast as possible!!! Party!!! This is human nature.

Why Separate, Named Savings Accounts?

The simple reason we need multiple savings accounts is that we humans are a lot less likely to raid a savings account with a name on it.

Here's a common post-college scenario. Two of your best friends just got engaged, and you know what that means. The parties, the travel, the gifts, etc. And you don't make squat for money at the moment. So, you open a savings account immediately to start siphoning a little away each month. At the same time, your car's last mile of existence is imminent. It is very clear that a car purchase, however modest, is on the horizon.

If you open a savings account with both of those in mind, what will happen? Well, whichever "event" comes first will get to rob the whole thing. The intensity and need of that moment will make you conveniently forget that you have purposes for that account.

On the flip side, if you have separate, named accounts for each of those, you will be far less likely to do that. You know the intensity of need for each. Plus, you will fund them enough. Sometimes those compiled savings accounts can get large, and you can mistakenly think you are *so* rich! Maybe you can more easily back off funding so aggressively because there is "plenty" there. It's only after you sift through the account that you realize you have barely enough for the purposes you are saving for. Mind games are powerful.

The beauty of getting into a habit with a cash flow system like this is that it can become a lifetime system for you now, and if you partner, for you as a couple. The system is the same, but the purposes change.

Let's say you are now married and decide to buy a new sectional that will cost $3,000, but you don't have the money. Are you going to take it out of the family vacation account? Nope—that thing is planned and booked. Money can't come from there! Are you going to take it out of your kids' college education? No. Maybe those kids did talk back that morning but let's face it, you still love 'em. Will you take it out of your dream fund for starting a business? No way!

There might still be a way to get that sectional that we will discuss later, but the point is that your dream funds will likely stay safely deposited in their individual savings accounts, even in the face of tempting, last-minute purchases. I recommend that you save for these dreams explicitly, just like your retirement, or you will find those dreams whittled away year after year.

There was a shocking story in the May 2016 *Atlantic Monthly*, which revealed that in a Fed survey 47% of people answered that they could not come up with $400 in an emergency. Importantly, they noted that "they would cover the expense by borrowing or selling something, or they would not be able to come up with the $400 at all."[41] That is financially terrifying. But one thing I loved about the story is that the author goes on to reveal that he is in that 47%. We catch a glimpse into Neal Gabler's life, living paycheck to paycheck, but never guessing as observers that it could ever be the case. Many of us live from paycheck to paycheck or have done so in the past. Me included. But science tells us that it is not a coincidence. It is our natural human adaptation once again rearing its head. We have learned to adapt to the changing circumstances of our bodies, food supplies, and other natural challenges.

When it comes to money, we naturally adapt. There is no universal lifestyle to which we benchmark.

I was recently asked to write an expert piece in a high-end lifestyle magazine. They said the average annual income of the targeted readership was $200,000, so I wrote the budget for that amount. Outrage followed. People who earned less than $200,000 per year could not even imagine a need to budget when you had that much money. Those folks could save piles of money if they wanted to. Let's assume that the average income for the outraged people was $100,000 per year. Half. For them, that extra after-tax money of around $60,000 could shore up a comfortable retirement, ensure their kids' college education, and defend against emergencies.

But, would that happen? If someone making $100,000 were suddenly to make $200,000, would the extra $60,000 naturally go into savings? Doubtful.

I think often about a single dad in one of my retirement plans who made just over minimum wage. On the weekends he worked odd jobs to help pay the bills. He was a 10% saver. I asked him why he had been doing it at that level for so long, and he said that even though he made so little he understood that he was the only one who would ever take care of himself or his three kids. From his research, he knew 10% would be enough to support himself in retirement. He also revealed an emergency fund that had several thousand in it. Every time I came back to that office, he was reading a financial book. He knew about adaptation, and though he lived on unimaginably low wages, through intense planning and vigilance he had more savings than many people who made 10 times his pay.

How many times have I had someone in my office say that they could save if they only made a little more money? Answer: almost always. Here's the funniest truth: I still find myself thinking it. *If I only made . . . we could do . . .*

I want to acknowledge here that many people in our country do not make enough money. It is the truth. With high insurance deductibles and expensive childcare, the numbers do not add up for making minimum wage and affording these things while also buying food and putting roofs over their heads. And while I applaud my single dad for being able to find his path to financial stability, I would not judge someone else in his shoes who couldn't. What is the line? I do not know. All I can do is shine a light for folks who want to find their financial stability and might have just the means to do it. In the meantime, we need to figure out how to deal with these rising costs so that people who don't make much money can live with dignity.

For many of us, the reality is that more money will not fund our dreams, or our retirement, or bring us more joy or contentment. Studies repeatedly support these findings, that people need "enough" money to feel joy and contentment. But, surprisingly, the increases over the "enough" amount do not raise feelings of joy or contentment. Increases that become significantly greater than the "enough" amount can actually have the opposite effect, which is to remove joy and contentment from that person's life.

More money will give you more problems if you don't manage it proactively. More money means a more expensive lifestyle that you will have to support throughout life and through a potentially longer retirement (we are living longer, and women generally outlive men). When we get used to things being a certain way, tightening the belt can feel like deprivation and we humans don't like to feel deprived. More money with less planning does not make people happier. I have experienced this repeatedly with clients who thought more money was the answer—it was not.

So, if you *plan* for more money before there *is* more money and shuttle that more money into these meaningful savings accounts, you get to stop the pesky adaptation process before it starts. We have done this cash flow process with people who had inflated their lifestyles with their pay, and I can report back from these experiences that it is much harder to reduce a lifestyle than to set the ideal one in the first place. So, hint hint, nudge nudge. Do not delay!

Choosing Your Accounts

We are going to walk through the accounts that I find are the most common. For many young people, setting up two to three accounts, like emergency fund, car, and travel can be enough. You might find that six or seven accounts resonate. If so, set them up. Err on the side of too many accounts.

Before you can calculate monthly amounts to go into savings, you will need to know your net pay. To get from our Step 1: Pay Yourself First to Step 2, we have to acknowledge the taxes and deductions that reduce our gross pay to solve for our net pay. The net paycheck is what we will use to derive our spendable income for Steps 2 through 4 of the system. There are a couple of options for figuring this out:

1. Call HR and ask them to run a sample paycheck for you based on contributing 10% to your retirement account.

2. Use a paycheck calculator to simulate what it would look like. Here's one: www.calculator.net/take-home-pay-calculator.html

3. If you are following along in the cash flow worksheet at ButFirstSave10.com, you can enter that net pay as your starting cash for Step 2.

Taxes & Deductions

Pay Yourself First

***** TAXES & DEDUCTIONS *****

**There isn't a decision that we have
to make about TAXES & DEDUCTIONS, but
they do affect our net (take-home) pay.**

Emergency Fund

Back to emergency funds, the most important savings account of all. I asked you to make an emergency fund before, and this is me reinforcing the ask. There are very few times that I am dogmatic in financial planning, but building an emergency fund is a must. So far, money has been fun, exciting, and glamorous. The emergency fund, by its nature, seems the opposite of that. Why, you might ask? Because we call it the worst name ever! Emergency fund! Follow me here—the nature of emergencies is that they come up unexpectedly. Given that I "unexpect" (*can I make up that word?*) an emergency, why would I ever have an emergency fund?

This is where you get to flip the script, change the narrative. First of all, whatever you want to label it, this is a pile of cash, and let's recognize the power of a woman backed by a pile of her own cash.

Fortunately, I also find that, for the most part, when the topic comes up my clients agree, and many have indeed started their own emergency funds. The only issue with the emergency fund is that it typically gets raided when money is needed for an assortment of reasons already highlighted above. But here is the thing—the scary unknown, while rare, takes money. Lots of money. And you must have it. If you get sick and cannot work, you will need money to replace lost wages. If you don't have it, then in the middle of getting sick, you might have to move out of your home, sell your possessions, or borrow from friends and family. Prolonged poor health, divorce, litigation, natural disasters, death of someone close to you, or job loss will rock your world. Money is what is needed to weather that Category 5 hurricane.

When you make an emergency fund, it needs to have three to six months of monthly expenses in it. Put it in a savings account called "emergency," and do not use it. If you must ask whether something is an emergency, by its very definition it is not. Don't use it and look elsewhere. Trust me. You will know an emergency when you see it. I have never in my career seen more people facing the reality of spending down their emergency funds than in 2020 because of the pandemic. I keep returning to update the numbers because tens of millions have lost their jobs. For many people, this is an emergency.

I also recommend that the calculation of the emergency fund be based on three to six months of spending, not gross pay, but take-home pay. Let's think about Olivia the saver and Olivia the spending, both making $45,000 per year. Olivia the saver puts 10% into retirement and 5% into paying her student loans. Olivia the spender saves nothing and spends everything. In an emergency situation, what will Olivia need to come up with? Logically, two different amounts. For Olivia the saver, 31.7% was going into taxes and benefits and 10% into retirement. That leaves spending of 58%, or $2,188 per month. To have six months saved up would require around $13,000. For Olivia the spender, 31.7% was going into taxes and benefits and nothing into retirement. This leaves 68.3%, or $2,562 required to keep her lifestyle going. The total amount for 6 months would be over $15,000.

A lot of people get hung up on the actual amount to keep in an account, when the real issue most people face is how to build up any amount at all. Sometimes building an emergency fund is the most painful form of saving, which is why it is most often neglected, or why people will so easily repurpose it into a credit card overflow account, the backup home repair reserve, or the new alternator fund. None of those things are inherently an emergency, but, funny enough, the lack of funds to pay them *make them an emergency*. Hence why you would start other savings accounts besides the emergency fund.

You can do this! You need to do this. Build it one time, then you never have to do it again. That is, unless you get a huge pay raise, in which case building the emergency fund would be pretty fast and easy since you are making more money. My advice is to be realistic. First, check into whether there are any windfalls coming up in the next year, such as a tax refund, inheritance, bonus, or side business income. But most people don't have that. Olivia needs to build an emergency fund of $13,000, but her contribution schedule and amounts need to be realistic. It probably isn't going to happen very fast, but while Olivia is

Save for Emergencies

Pay Yourself First

***** TAXES & DEDUCTIONS *****

SAVE FOR EMERGENCIES

Action item

Open a savings account not linked to your main checking.
Auto-transfer savings each month until you have 3-6 months
of expenses saved.

living at home she will put $300 per month into the account. Luckily, when building an emergency fund in the context of this system, finding an affordable monthly deposit is possible. Remember, this is all part of a larger iterative process that includes personal customization, some trial and error, but above all else, a necessary beginning.

Here is where I would start.

If any parents happen to be reading this book and are wondering about a good way to help kids get a head start on a financial plan, creating an emergency fund is a great way to start (hint, hint).

☑ **ACTION:** Open a savings account. If you work for a company that can payroll deduct your savings into a separate savings account, consider opening an online high-yield savings account. This could be at Ally, Synchrony Bank, or American Express. Every pay period, have your emergency fund amount automatically deposited, so you never see the money. Try to forget you have that account! If you do not have the ability to payroll deduct into an outside account, then you are better off setting up the savings account linked to your checking. Arrange a monthly auto transfer from your checking account to the savings account. But trust me, better call that emergency fund somethin' cool to keep you from robbing it!

Travel

Do me a favor. Commit to staying in your home, your town, your state, your country for 10 years. Right now. Do it.

If you recoiled at that statement, then get on your running shoes and sprint to the nearest bank to set up a travel savings account. Think money can't bring happiness? Think again. Vacations are proven to elevate happiness.

Now, raise your hand if you don't have the money but take the vacation anyway. Before booking that flight, you've said something like,

"You only live once," or maybe justified it because you work really hard. By the way, both statements are probably true. It doesn't matter how deserved or desired or part of your DNA travel is, if you don't have the money, you don't take the trip. If you do, then this is a trip-on-debt.

The trip-on-debt hangover, in my opinion, negates the benefit of the trip. No matter what you might see on Instagram, it's what I see in my office when the sum total of trips-on-debt weighs on marriages, limits the ability to retire, and causes acute short-term (and often long-term) credit card bills that have to be repaid. Think about it, if you didn't have the money to take the trip in the first place, then how are you going to have the money to pay for the trip in the second place? You won't. You have to spend maybe the next six months to a year paying *more*, maybe much more, than the trip originally cost because you then have to pay the interest on the credit card.

Logically, do you think it would be easier to pay for a trip in *anticipation* of it or *after* the trip is over?

Yet, we Americans continue to take trips and pay for them later. Over and over and over again. Why do you think airlines are cramming credit cards down our throats in airports or even *on the airplane*? Because they know people are big spenders when it comes to travel. They know you will not likely save for travel ahead of time and that your brain will light up at the notion of "miles" which might enhance your spending. All this is a perfect recipe for the airlines to earn interest. There are plenty of offers for lots of sick, beautiful, free money. Mostly sick. Think of it that way—as a germy mess that will infect your life and make you sick, too.

There is a better way, and it is so simple. Save for vacations. And then take them.

Yes, this savings account serves two purposes. It keeps us from going into debt on vacations (which negates the benefit) *and* it helps us take vacations. You heard me. I am actually telling you to spend money. Also, it reminds us in the shorter term how wonderful we are for doing this saving thing because we want to do something awesome and, because we've planned, we are free to do it. This is a little taste of the freedom that lies ahead in retirement.

Many people argue the case against budgeting as living more fully in the now. There is a perception that we have to completely delay all comforts and happiness to the future. This could not be further from the truth. Managing money is about balancing the future and the now. Recall that if you start that balance early enough in life, it is a very small sacrifice to make—just 10% to put in a time capsule and send to your future. After that, spend it all. But please be sure to spend it on what's going to bring security, peace, and joy first. Setting up these savings accounts and funding them automatically for emergencies, travel, and other things you value are how you make sure those priorities are funded first.

What if you sat down and dreamed of all the vacations, large and small, that you would take in the next two years? Are there friends you would visit? Do you have an international trip on your bucket list? Add them all up, and then divide it by the period of time. For Olivia, it's a trip to visit friends in California ($900), a camping trip ($150), and a Caribbean cruise ($1,200) with her college friends over 2 years. That's $2,250 total. If she divides that by 24 months, she needs to save $93.75 per month. Is that affordable? If so, she should bank it! Have you figured out your amount? Then open up an account, call it something festive like "travel" or "vacations" or "getaways." Name it something too fabulous to rob. Then set up an auto transfer from your checking account to that savings account.

In 2018, we had increased our savings ahead of a trip to my husband's home country of Colombia for a large family reunion. His father is one of 14 children! We thought it would be more expensive, but with some flight itinerary maneuvers and much less expensive housing and food than we had expected, there was money left over. With the savings, we were able to book a trip to see my best friend in Phoenix for her baby shower and then have the trip of a lifetime in Sedona as a family.

The account balance was the only reason we booked that trip. With 3 kids in tow, it is often easier for my husband and me to stay at home. The money in the account actually *encouraged* us to spend the money, and if it was just in a general account, I promise it would have been whittled away on clothes or even something "responsible."

This is what I want for you. It's the ability to get out of town, see something new, go to a new country, get a fresh perspective. Go see those red rocks in Sedona. They are waiting for you!

☑ **ACTION:** Set up a savings account attached to your checking account, and label it "travel," "vacation," or the name that makes the most sense to you. After you calculate your savings dreams that you can afford each month, set up an auto transfer from your checking account to your new savings account. Set it up on the 3rd to the 5th of the month to make sure it's late enough for your paycheck to hit your checking account but early enough to get the money out of the checking account before you spend it.

Weddings and Baby Showers

Give me just a quick second. I need to go dig around in my closet for my "judgmental" hat. It's there somewhere. Okay, found it. Don't worry—this isn't directed at you, so please indulge me for a minute. Let me dust it off, and then we can get started. Dusted!

Women in their 20s (men, also, but to a lesser extent) are going broke celebrating their friends' weddings and baby showers. Does this budget seem crazy? A bridesmaid dress at $250, shoes at $75, gift at $100, flight at $400, room at $150 and destination bachelorette party at $400. That's a $1,375 price tag. Consider Olivia making $45,000 per year. Her available money to spend after savings, taxes, and student loan payments is $1,818 a month. That's before she has paid rent (after she moves out of her parents' house), groceries, cell phone usage, gym membership, or charitable giving. I promise, THIS IS CRAZY. It makes no sense. And, this sucker is rinse and repeat because she could have one wedding in the spring and two in the fall. Then, she has to be ready to do it again the next year.

I can't tell you how many women end up in my office beating themselves up because they have a credit card bill they can't pay and haven't started their 401(k) plan at work yet, leaving behind all the free money the company wants to hand them.

Yes, I judge. I judge the whole thing. We (as a society) have created a box for what a wedding looks like. Instagram demands a large wedding party for the sea of faces in carefully curated photos. And while everyone should have the wedding of their dreams, I don't think any bride would care to witness her bridesmaid in my office wringing her hands in worry and think this is all normal and something she would willingly do to her friend.

But no one talks about money or raises the issue of affordability, so the cycle of pain continues.

This is me bringing it up. This is me asking you, bride, to do some rough math of what your wedding would cost your dear friends who will say "yes" to whatever you ask them to do.

This is me asking you, bridesmaid, to consider saying "no." Maybe not to being a bridesmaid but perhaps to a dress that costs more than $100, the shoes that cost that much and won't show under the dress, or the trip that costs hundreds of dollars or more. Or, what about just saying that because you have reached your budget, you won't be able to give her something from her registry? You could make or do or write something sentimental that will mean even more. Say "no" to some or most of it, and I promise your courage will be so appreciated by other members of the wedding party. Saying no early can help you spend time with the bride finding some shortcuts or workarounds. If she is a true friend, she will understand, and if she does not, well . . .

Brides, please, bring this up with your bridesmaids. Tell them you want to make this experience fun and not leave your dearest friends with that stressful debt hangover afterwards. Figure out what is the most important. If it is a certain look you want and the dresses you are sold on are $350, consider subsidizing. If it is being together, then prioritize that expense.

My friend had a destination wedding, and she went to such appreciated lengths to figure out how everyone could afford it. She booked homes that when split up by room were less than $100 per night. She had everyone caravan from Phoenix to Rocky Point, Mexico. She paid for people to cook most of the meals onsite at the homes we stayed in instead of having meals out. Bridesmaid dresses were beautiful and affordable, and we got to be barefoot on the beach. Everyone who attended had the benefit of time with each other and a truly breathtaking beach vacation. It was a win-win and showed me that there was a way around society's pressures to spend so much money and ask others to spend so much money surrounding nuptials.

Now to babies. Throwing baby showers can also be pricey (but I will say showers are my favorite parties to throw). The best advice I have is to host them in a home and join up with several people to defray the cost and increase the help (not to mention great ideas). I have noticed in my personal experience co-hosting events that, as a group, we tended to underestimate expenses, even though I'm a financial planner. I think this is a pretty common phenomenon. And it's really the last-minute things that can get you—the extra decorations the group thinks up, the freak-out moment when you worry there's not enough food and buy extra, hiring the housekeeper, etc. Make a budget and stick to the budget.

Finally, if you are asked to join in and co-host a party to the tune of $300, not including a gift, and you are making $45,000 a year, you might have to decline. That is simply not available to you, by any stretch, and you can own this. Maybe instead, if your schedule allows, you can offer to spend the hours before the party picking up the cake, getting the gifts wrapped, checking on the catering, etc. You'd be surprised how many people find time more valuable than money, so it might be worth asking.

Let's sidebar for a second. Everyone is struggling with budgets. I can tell you from my meetings that $300 can derail even someone making $300,000 per year. Becoming a financial planner after being someone who struggled with money has liberated me tremendously. I have had hundreds of personal conversations about money so am almost completely desensitized to the taboo nature of discussing money. And let me tell you very few people actually feel like they can go around without a care in the world when it comes to money. Yes, I know. It seems like they can. It seems like they can whip out that credit card at a high-end boutique and buy something mindlessly, but very few people can do this. The Range Rovers and the fancy nurseries, all of it, were costs at the expense of other things or to the tune of credit card debt.

The point is, I want you to feel liberated to boldly discuss your budget. If you are in your 20s, you probably are broke and societally can own being broke. One of my favorite stories is a young business executive who proudly lived in a small apartment, shared a car with a friend, and often walked to work. Why did she choose to live so modestly? She had a lot of student loan debt and decided to pour all those pay raises and bonuses into her eventual freedom from all that debt. Did walking to work or living in a small apartment impact her career? I guess we have no counterfactual, but I haven't met many executives who were so young. Her work spoke for itself, not a perception of success.

These are the years to start from the bottom rung and work your way up. If you are driving around in a nice car in your 20s, very few people think you are successful. They assume someone bought you that car. So, feel liberated to drive the clunker. Wear second-hand clothes. Own your broke-ness. Tell the broke-ness to friends and family. There is something romantic about it, in fact. What you might find on the other end of the explanation is not horrified gasps but sighs of relief. You might open the door to hearing the stories I hear all day long. We are all trying to figure out how to get by, and the pressure to have it all (or buy it all) is too much.

(Slowly and reluctantly removes judgmental hat and walks it back up to the attic.)

☑ **ACTION:** If you anticipate being in lots of weddings or are in baby shower season, please set up a savings account just for these events. Get a realistic budget as soon as possible and divide the expected spending by the time remaining before the event. Then, auto draft that amount from your account every month until the event. If a wedding, all in, is expected to cost $900, and you have 7 months to save, then you need to auto transfer $128 per month into your "wedding and/or baby" savings account.

Health Savings Accounts (HSAs)

Health savings accounts are necessary, really really necessary, for people who have what are called HDHPs (high-deductible healthcare plans). You might have a traditional health insurance plan that has a very low deductible or no deductible, and you pay for health visits or procedures with co-payments. While those can still be crippling, they don't tend to be as disruptive to personal finances as high deductible healthcare plans. That's why we will focus narrowly on HDHPs. If you have an HSA-eligible plan, then you absolutely must set up an HSA and fund it just like these other savings accounts. Thankfully, your company can help you set it up and it may even go an extra step and help fund the HSA.

I am going to divvy this discussion up into two sections. The first is survival in the Wild West of healthcare. Most of you will happily stay right there. The second section is for people who have high incomes, like physicians. You will look at the HSA less as survival and more as another tax-efficient savings account for retirement. Yes, I said retirement. Stick with me.

Healthcare Survival

Healthcare may truly be the least sexy thing to discuss regarding finances, but this ain't your grandparent's healthcare anymore, kids. Think *The Hunger Games*. This dark, Darwinian game will bring you to your knees, especially if you dare to choose a noble profession like a teacher or laborer. If you are on your parents' healthcare plan until the age of 26, drop them a note of thanks every now and then. This comes at great expense to them.

Why is this a dark reality? For 2 reasons. The first is how much you have to pay for something that you are not likely to consume. You could pay hundreds of dollars in premiums every month and literally never go to the doctor. This is the good, lucky dark. You pay a lot of money to subsidize other people's healthcare in a badly broken healthcare system. The second dark reason is how badly you get punished for losing the health lottery. God forbid you have type 1 diabetes or a heart condition, because you will pay those premiums you can barely afford *plus* you will pay your deductible, co-insurance, and ultimately out-of-pocket maximum—or "OOPs."

What if you don't get insured? Bad idea. Just a really, really bad idea. Everyone needs health insurance. Period. Take a tumble while snowboarding for the first time or have an expensive chronic illness? You still have to pay, even if you don't have the money.

Before I get too far onto my soap box, let's get some jargon out of the way. There are three pieces of healthcare jargon that you must understand, unequivocally. The first is deductible, the second is co-insurance, and the third is out-of-pocket. Other people might tell you other jargon is just as important, but I gotta tell you, when you live in District 13 of The *Hunger Games* (before the uprising), these are the only 3three things that can suck really bad. A deductible is the amount you must pay before the plan pays anything for your claims (with the exception of preventive care). Once you meet your deductible in a calendar year, the plan will pay covered claims subject to you paying a certain percentage. Your share is called co-insurance. Finally, there is a maximum amount you will have to pay in a given year. This is called the out-of-pocket maximum.

Let's use an example. Did you know that even if you pay hundreds of dollars in premiums, that one kickball game gone bad and your torn ACL could cost you $8,000? See, what happens is that you first hit your deductible of $7,000, meaning every single healthcare expense you incur will be paid by you. Yes, you. But some of your expenses, even after you hit the deductible, will not be picked up by insurance 100%. Instead, they are paid through co-insurance in which you and the insurance company are co-insurers—the company will pay 50% of all expenses but you still have to pay the remaining 50%. Relief does not come until you, yourself, and your checkbook have written checks in one year totaling $8,150. That is your out-of-pocket maximum, or, again, the "OOPs." Then, finally, the health insurance pays 100% of the costs.

Uncle.

Let's apply this scenario to Olivia. Her take-home pay after student loans is $1,817. Suddenly, she is on the hook for $8,150/12, or a payment plan to pay $679 per month for a year because of that ACL surgery. Oh. My. God.

Folks, when I see a GoFundMe or FB fundraiser for some family or individual that has hit healthcare calamity, I donate. Healthcare, until our system is fixed, is a village endeavor. When you see a family raising money to pay a health "OOPs," it is no joke. The lucky among us who are healthy need to throw $15 to $30 into the pot. It's not a scam. These people are having to deal with the stress of illness or accident, and finances are an added stress that should not be there in the darkest of days.

This chapter is not a political statement. It is a wake-up call. If you live in America, you may suffer when it comes to healthcare unless you are very, very rich (and thus these healthcare expenses are a rounding error). If your health lottery number comes up, it's not a matter of whether you will suffer. It's by degree of magnitude you will suffer. And the earlier you come to face the reality of this, the better. So, either figure out how to get really rich or start building up a healthcare war chest immediately. You literally cannot afford to make a mistake. Not one.

Paying premiums either happens through pre-tax deductions out of your paycheck, or if you own a business or are a gig worker then you would pay premiums below in the "bills" section. Assuming you make a life budget of your bills before you make major decisions like how much house or car to buy, you should be fine in that department. But the killer you need to defend against is the OOPs. God forbid you experience an OOPs. Some people go through life thinking that prayer will prevent an OOPs, but I know plenty of God-fearing folks who get side-swiped by a cancer diagnosis or slip and fall the wrong way. Nice idea. Doesn't work.

The moment you sign up for your health insurance, just look for the number next to "out of pocket." THAT is your health savings goal, and you need to hit that number as quickly as possible, hopefully in a year or two. Let's say your OOPs is $10,000; you need to save $400-$800 per month for a year until you have that buffer.

Where to save it is interesting. You can save into a regular savings account for these other savings goals, but for healthcare it's a little different. The federal government has an account for you if you have one of these high deductible healthcare plans. Literally, that's the name of it—a high-deductible healthcare plan, or HDHP. Sometimes they will say "HSA-eligible." In this case, you have the right to open and deposit into a health savings account through your company if it is offered, through your bank, or through some online HSA providers. The advantage is that up to a certain limit, the federal government lets you get a tax deduction on that money. Depending on your tax bracket, this means you could be getting a 12% to 24%+ deduction on whatever savings you put into the HSA. But that savings account has to be used on healthcare.

Importantly, an HSA is different from a flexible spending account, or an FSA. FSAs are the lottery-like "use it or lose it" accounts that send people to CVS buying Band-Aids and cough syrup at the end of the year to prevent losing all the money they had saved. Instead, HSAs can be fully funded and then not ever spent.

If you have a high-deductible plan, you must fund your HSA. In the same way your healthcare premium must get paid every month, you absolutely must fund your HSA every month.

You can visit ButFirstSave10.com for the latest on where to find an HSA, HSA limits or, even better, announcements if the moment ever arrives when Congress can actually figure out what to do with healthcare. Don't hold your breath for the last one; in the mean-time, unfortunately, it is up to you to protect yourself.

☑ **ACTION:** Find out if you have an HSA-eligible health-care plan. If so, find out what your out-of-pocket amount is, divide the amount by 12 (24 at the most, if your goal is to save the amount over 2 years), and set up an auto draft into your qualified HSA account for the amount. This can be done most conveniently at your company if it is offered there through pay-roll deduction.

HSA as a Retirement Account

For high-income folks, saving enough for retirement can be trickier. It's not as simple as picking the right percentage and saving that into the retirement plan. The federal government sets a max for it, and hitting that max could mean undersaving for retirement.

My company loves the HSA as another retirement account. Contributions go in tax-free, and, as long as money is spent on healthcare, the contributions don't get taxed on the back end. In addition, contributions can be invested in stocks and bonds, and none of the gains are taxed as long as money is used for health expenses. For this reason it has a *triple tax advantage*.

The strategy for you is to max out your HSA contribution through work (learn more on saving and investing in HSAs at ButFirstSave10.com) if your workplace offers an HSA that has the ability to be invested in stocks and bonds. If not, contribute to an HSA on your own and put as much as you can in it up to federal funding limits (minus what the company contributes to your HSA). In 2020, the maximum for an individual to contribute is $3,550 and for a family is $7,100.

Then don't spend it. That money can be invested in stocks and bonds inside your HSA and then when you go to retire, it's like having another retirement account, only better. When you take that money out to pay for health expenses in retirement, you don't have to pay taxes on that money. Literally, the only dollars you will ever have that you didn't pay taxes on in your whole life (ahem—we won't mention the babysitting money when you were a teen). Oh, and by the way, what's the number one expense in retirement? You got it—healthcare.

Open up a separate savings account, call it "health", and contribute enough to be able to cover any OOPs.

☑ **ACTION:** Start an HSA and max out the contribution alongside the employer. Then invest it in stocks and bonds for retirement. Open a separate savings account at your bank to cover healthcare expenses that may arise. Set up an auto transfer for the healthcare you anticipate using, or take your "OOPs" and divide by 12 to fund your savings. Use that savings account, not your HSA, for expenses.

Gifts

I happen to be writing this section at the end of the year. The Christmas hangover is in full effect, and I realize that, yet again, we have far eclipsed our "budget" for gifts. By several hundred dollars.

Where did the money go? Each month, we auto transfer what I consider the craziest sum of money into a savings account. It goes to birthday gifts and parties, teacher gifts, housewarming gifts, wedding and baby shower gifts, charitable donations, and, finally, Christmas. We have increased this budget every year, and yet it is never ever enough. I just don't understand.

But when I go back and look over it all, there is little I would change. Generosity is important to me, and it's probably important to you. I have already scaled down my gifting sizes/amounts to what fits our actual budget. We literally stopped throwing kid birthday parties. What starts out as "Oh yeah, it should cost about $250 to throw our kid a birthday" turns into $250 for the kid venue rental, $30 for napkins/plates/decorations, $50 for the pizzas, $50+ for the cake, $25 for junk party favors that will be dumped into every crevice of every minivan that departs the party, $50 for a gift, etc. Suddenly your $250 party, at the low end, is $455. Then you multiply that by 3 kids and realize that to throw all your kids "affordable" birthday parties comes to $1,365. (You might say, "Throw it at home." NO. WAY.)

Our alternative is that we now plan birthdays to coincide with travel or experiences. Think of all you could do with $1,365!

Here are some other ideas:

- Instead of gifts for friends on birthdays or other milestones, go to dinner. It's something you would enjoy doing anyway.

- Look at all the Christmas or other holiday events and see where you could start planning earlier in the year. One friend volunteered to coordinate her child's classroom gift budget at the beginning of the school year with people contributing at their comfort level. It was a win-win with a nicer gift for the teacher and the last-minute dash within the more expensive holiday-time window eliminated.

- Maybe just throw a birthday party every three or so years, and give the gift of a cool experience on the in-between years (like a day at a theme park) with a friend.

- Call off all gifts for adults around holidays. No one needs anything. If they did, they would go buy it. You might feel like Scrooge doing it, but once you bring it up everyone is so relieved. Imagine how much incremental enjoyment everyone would have without that stress and pressure. We still draw names as a family, which is an improvement, but I would love for us to get to the point of no gifts at all.

My son recently asked my husband if he was going to buy me a diamond bracelet—something he had seen in a commercial. Jorge and I both laughed, and Jorge jokingly said I would have to find another husband for that.

We don't exchange gifts. It is a deep pact we have with each other to buy what we need or want for ourselves, subject to our means. Instead of gifts, we experience. We will both take the day off on a birthday or anniversary and spend the day together, going to meals and playing hooky while the kids are at school. We both own our own businesses and call our own shots. We live the lives we once dreamed of. No diamond bracelet could replace the feeling of owning our own time and the ability to take a day off and just enjoy it together. More importantly, what's missing is not the diamond bracelet, rather the debt hangover. What is gained in place of the diamond bracelet is the the freedom of our time.

Aside from the big events like weddings, baby showers, birthday parties, and holidays, what hits people's budgets so hard is the volume of gifts. It's the sheer quantity of all the gifts, even when you don't have kids, like Administrative Professionals Day, Mother's Day, Father's Day, etc., times infinity. And it is unavoidable to most people. I find people are *shocked* when they do expense analyses and find out just how much they spent on gifts in a year. It can be a large point of contention with spouses.

My best advice is to save and plan where you can. Then, face the reality and siphon the money away. The issue with gift giving is that you have to save for the larger, "lumpier" expenses, while at the same time shelling out for smaller gifts throughout the year. The best way to do this is to set up a gift budget and look at the last year of expenses. Tally up all the gifts you gave last year and look at any family or friends' weddings or babies that might be imminent in the next year. Put it in the budget. The thing is, unless you can honest-to-goodness say you will refuse to buy a gift, then you must prepare for it. And so much better to put away for it regularly than to get hit hard episodically.

☑ **ACTION:** Open a savings account called "gifts." Estimate what gifts will cost through the year and divide by 12. Auto transfer that monthly amount from your main checking account into the gift account.

Technology

There is not a lot to say about this account, and in full disclosure I do not have a technology account. But I do have clients who have them. Think about whether you are a technology early adopter, in the line for the newest iPhone, even if you just bought one a year ago. Do you have a tech-enabled home with voice-enabled lights, a doorbell that can catch neighbors' street bloopers, or nine kids that each get an iPad? If so, add it all up. If you spend $2,000, on average, each year in tech upgrades then you should seriously consider putting $167 per month into a savings account for these purchases.

Yep, nearly a car payment.

☑ **ACTION:** If you are a tech junky (or someone who breaks/cracks/loses their phone annually), start up a savings account called "tech" and deposit a monthly portion of a year's worth of estimated expenses. Make a list of all your tech, how much it costs, and how many years to replace it. Divide the cost by the number of years and then add up those costs to get a yearly estimate. Divide that by 12 to get cost on a monthly basis. That is how much you should auto transfer from your main checking account into your tech savings account.

Cars

What I am about to propose is downright un-American. I am going to suggest that you save for your next car and pay in cash.

Society puts cars in the bills section. We have been lulled, hypnotized, coerced into believing that car payments are a fact of life. And meeting after meeting, another stressed-out young person wants desperately to save . . . when their car gets paid off. In five years. No, they can't sell it. It's underwater. It's safe. There's nothing else they can drive.

So, you can see where I stand on cars. I love cars and dream of that Tesla, remember? There are people who build their financial plans on the feat of driving a car to 250,000 miles. Awesome. Love it. But that's them. It's not me. It may not be you.

Here's what needs to happen. You need to save for your next car. Then go buy it in cash. I know, I know. "But the low interest rate" they say. "The sick money and the debt hangover!" I reply. Yep, I have heard it all. I have vetted it all. And I am telling you without a doubt that I am one of the few loving, caring people who do not want to sentence you to a car payment.

Go open that account. Call it "car." And put your own car payment in it.

Maybe you are not convinced. Let's try something else. Go look at some cars right now with a budget in mind—call it $25,000—and watch your brain start lighting up. When you find the car you like, see what the 60-month loan would be. Based on what I have been seeing recently and assuming you have good enough credit for a 7% interest loan, it's probably going to be about $500 per month. Watch yourself start doing the mental gymnastics to convince yourself that you can make it work. You can "stretch" your dollars. After all, for just $500, look at that ride! It's going to have a push start and fabulous new-smelling leather and the most beautiful technology interface. It has side-curtain airbags and other features that make it safer for your kids or those you may have in the forseeable future. It's only $500. What a no-brainer.

Now, go find someone you know with a nearly 5-year-old car that cost about $25,000 when they bought it. Go sit in it. Test drive it. Breathe in the familiar scent of the athletic gym bag that sits in the back seat, the cup of two-day-old Starbucks latte with festering milk in the cupholder, and the Chick-fil-A fries that fell into no man's land between the driver's seat and the armrest. Try hooking up to the Bluetooth only to realize that it doesn't really work that well. Try and appreciate the sound of the "vintage" speakers compared to the crystal-clear speakers in the new car.

Now, get ready. You still get to pay $500 per month for this car.

But you are sick of this car. You can't stand it. You want the new car. Coincidentally, the dealer just sent a handwritten note telling you there is this incredible deal. They have too many new cars on the lot just like yours and only for loyal customers like yourself are offering the chance to keep your payment the same and get that new car.

And the clock resets. Five more years.

I hope you are convinced that the car story does not play out in the fairy tale we have been told our whole lives, so you entertain the option to buy in cash. Of course, it's no fun. After some back and forth, you agree that *maybe* you could afford to put $200 per month into a savings account. And you automate it. And five years later you have $12,000.

Ok, it's time to buy the car. You walk right past the new $25,000 cars and ask for the used ones. Why? You know what's coming—the studies show it is way harder to spend your own money than other people's money. You saw that balance in the car fund grow painfully slow over time, from $200 to $400 to $600. You thought this day might never come. But it's here. And you are buying a real car with real money. And you are never, ever going to have a car payment again. That $12,000 ride suddenly is the most luxurious car on the lot. The license plate should read "freedom."

Insurance

Insurance is the most common expense for young people. Did you know that you can pay less money on your car insurance, like a lot less, by pre-paying it one time per year? In many instances it can cost 15% less, so savings can be hundreds of dollars. The problem is that for some people who pay this way, that annual payment can hurt quite a bit when they have to scramble to find the money. Or they call uncle and make it a monthly payment, resigning themselves to pay 15% more for the same protection.

I am probably a broken record at this point, but I highly recommend setting up an "insurance" savings account, dividing your annual premium by 12, and transferring that monthly amount into your savings each month. Then when it is time to write the check, or after it hits your credit card, you have the money in savings to reimburse your checking account.

You may have other similar bills to car insurance that you could save ahead for in the same account, such as homeowners insurance, property taxes on the home, personal property taxes on that new car (ahem) you just bought, etc.

☑ ACTION: If you have an annual insurance or tax payment, divide the amount you owe by 12 and set up an auto transfer from your master checking account into that savings account named "insurance" or even "insurance and property taxes."

Clothes and "Beauty"

Beauty is in the eye of the beholder, and when we look in the mirror, too often we only see the hurdles to beauty. (Bet you didn't know a money book was going to talk about *that*!) Enter the beauty industry, ready to make it easy for us to muster every attempt possible to leap over those hurdles . . . tossing bags of money over our shoulders as we leap. I hope by now you realize that while I do say lots of countercultural things, this girl is a spender. And I love me some beauty products. Every last commercial to slather on this, swallow those, or soak in that, I am in. Let's do this.

But then I run the math on these beauty regimens, some that cycle every six months here, monthly there. Then the facials and manicures and pedicures. Oh, and the haircuts and color (which feels less optional when grays sprout). Add it up for the year. Divide by 12. Even the frugal among us might gulp at a number that can be upwards of $100 per month.

Then there are clothes. It's super funny—not one client buys clothes. Not ever. In my expense reviews, that blank is typically zero. When I run numbers with my retirement plan participants, again, zero. They say, "Oh, I don't buy clothes." And I get it, neither do I. Until I buy clothes. Someone, please study and name this brain malfunction. Somehow, we can go to the grocery store and buy groceries. We emerge realizing we just spent $150 when we went in to pick up milk. But we go to our favorite local boutique and pick up a dress for the cocktail party, and that was a neutral event. It didn't happen.

Ok, so we've called out this brain malfunction. Now, instead of asking you how much you spend on clothes, I am going to ask you this: Will you commit to spending zero dollars on clothes over the next year? Nothing. Nada. Gala coming up? Nope, can't buy a dress. High

☞ **Pro Tip**

A friend had a great suggestion. She stopped all fashion magazine subscriptions years ago because she realized simply the act of looking creates a desire that wasn't there naturally/already. She did the same with e-blasts from clothing companies . . . unsubscribe!

school reunion? Sorry—not gonna look fabulous in that new jumpsuit you've been eyeing. Work flats getting a hole in the bottom? Patch it up with some Fix-a-Flat. (Just kidding, I think that only works for tires.)

I just woke up the clothing purchase region of the brain, right? You're going to buy clothes. I am going to buy clothes. So, let's put the dollar on it, knowing that we will not go over that amount. We can't spend any more than we save.

How we shop is going to fall into one of two camps. I fall into the camp of loving to look fashionable but not loving the process. Therefore, my process might happen twice a year. I save through the year, then I buy what I need, and my husband and I get what the kids need.

A lot of people don't relate to this and instead buy clothing year-round. If that is you, don't worry, you will find a home for your clothing purchases in Step 4.

Truly, I recommend doing a careful analysis of your past year or two of clothing and beauty expenses to get a realistic understanding of the year (not including regular weekly or monthly expenses—those go in a different area). Then, you know the drill by now, divide by 12, and get your monthly savings amount.

☑ **ACTION:** After an analysis of your spending for the past year on clothing and beauty, add up your expenses, divide by 12, and auto transfer that amount from your master checking account to your "clothing and beauty" account.

Homes

In my opinion, the single largest disrupter of a good financial plan (behind emergencies with no emergency fund) is home ownership. For some reason, home ownership has become this important rite of passage for people in their 20s to "adult" and "stop throwing money away in rent." Pause for a minute. When you factor in ALL the costs of home ownership (mortgage, insurance, taxes, moving expenses, selling expenses, roof, air conditioner, water heater, kitchen appliance repair and replacement, etc., etc., etc.) it is usually a toss-up. But then when you consider a stronger proclivity to want to decorate and make your own home feel like your own home via furnishings, remodeling, painting, landscaping and improvements, and on and on, then it really doesn't make sense financially. Where I think home ownership makes sense is buying a home that you are likely to live in for more than 10 years. Five years is the traditional "break even" point for selling without a loss, but for me the 10-year break-even is able to accommodate all the unaccounted-for costs of transitioning a home. You want to buy a home once you are settled into a job you love, know you are staying in a town for a long time, and know that you can remain comfortably for a long time and/or raise a family for a while in the home.

Maybe that's you right now. Yay! Do you have a fund started to save for the down payment on your home? Not yet? Ok, this is going to be one of the most fun accounts you will start. A lot of emotion gets tied into homeownership, and you will likely feel a lot of excitement and nostalgia as you build this fund. Many well-respected financial experts recommend putting 20% down on a house and signing a 15-year mortgage. I cannot agree more. First, 20% down means you get to avoid PMI, or private mortgage insurance. If you can't put 20% down, then you actually have to pay an *extra* fee until you get 20% equity! Huh??? Don't go there.

Let's do some math. Say you want to buy a $200,000 house. (Stop laughing, San Francisco residents). Twenty percent of $200,000 is $40,000. You want to buy the house in 5 years, so that would be $667 per month to put in a savings account every month for the next 5 years.

Home Repair Savings

Congratulations, you own a home! But wait, there's more. You may already be well-versed in the costs of the mortgage payment, which probably also wraps the homeowner's insurance and property taxes into one payment. But that's just the known monthly fee. If you haven't already, you need to make another savings payment for the expected repairs. You can calculate these roughly but will rarely know when they'll strike. This is why I want you to make that payment into its own savings account called "home repair." First, figure out how much you probably need to save to maintain your home over time. (I usually recommend saving 1% to 1.5% of the value of your home into an account every

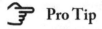

Pro Tip

For millennials, there is a big movement to pay your house off quickly. I don't have a problem with it. If you do pay off your house quickly, I recommend keeping a separate account for paying property taxes and insurance, in addition to maintaining the home repair account. When you have a mortgage, the mortgage company does this. It collects from your payment every month and "escrows" (what a funny, strange little duckling of a word to use in lieu of a simpler one called, um, saving) it. You can "escrow" that sucker yourself after the house gets paid off to avoid those "surprise" tax and insurance payments. Just get the annual insurance premium payment and the annual property tax bill/homeowners association bill and divide by 12 to get a monthly savings amount. Then when it is time to write the check, you have the money!

year.) Put that amount in a savings account each year. If you do that calculation, you very quickly realize that this is a lot of money. Even 1% of a $200,000 home is $2,000. Divide that by 12 and you need to squirrel away $167 per month.

But beware: This repair reserve does not include remodeling, renovation, or décor, just the basics to keep a home working properly. Again, not super glamorous and similar in psychological impact to the emergency fund. But, in the heat of the summer if your air conditioner goes out you will pay a lot of money to fix it. In fact, you'll pay pretty much whatever someone asks if you live in a part of the country where the temperatures routinely hover around 100 degrees! This savings account will give you peace of mind. You live in your home. You interact in your home all day long, and you are more aware of what can go wrong with it than anyone else. When I give talks to groups on this cash flow system, it's the home repair reserve where the whole audience starts nodding uncontrollably. Stuff goes wrong *all* the time, only now *you* are the "landlord," and there's no one else to call.

One more note on the home repair is that this is a separate savings concept from home remodeling. Home remodeling should be considered more of a "dream" or aspirational savings item. If you are constantly remodeling your home, remember that the market won't necessarily reward you for it. If you redo a kitchen that is only 10 years old, you have paid for two kitchens when the market will only pay you for one. When a home repair reserve hasn't been touched in a while and starts getting to $10,000 or higher, I have seen people want to use it for decorative purposes. You really must be clear and honest with yourself that it is purely for operational and maintenance purposes because just when you think you're ready to cash it in for some other use, major repairs *will* hit.

☑ **ACTION:** Set up an account called "home" or "home repair." Then set up an auto draft from your main checking account to your home repair account for 1% of the value of your home divided by 12 every month. Again, in our example, if your home is worth $200,000, then multiple by 1% to get $2,000. Divide by 12 to get $167. Auto transfer $167 per month from your main checking account into your home repair account.

☑ **ACTION if you DON'T own a home:** If you have a parent talking about "throwing money away in rent" then take a pic of this chapter with your phone and send it. You get to gleefully *not* open a home repair reserve if you don't own a home.

Kids: College Saving and Summer Activities

The moment your sweet new baby comes into the world—scratch that—the moment your sweet baby's social security card comes in the mail, I want you to run to your laptop and furiously, hastily sign up for a 529 college savings plan.

Let's do a quick down and dirty on this. If you are reading this section closely, then it applies to you, and I don't want to waste a single, bleary-eyed, stressed-out moment on ink you don't need.

Here's the thing. You will need to save for college. Yes, I promise. No matter how much of a genius junior is, this 529 will likely not go to waste (and, really, they don't go to waste, regardless). College is just too expensive. Period. We are talking about babies being born today expected to pay *hundreds of thousands* for college, and maybe just a little less than that if they get scholarships.

Where to save isn't controversial. If you pick something and save into it, great. Should you use a 529, a Roth, or a regular brokerage account? I personally use a 529 and think most people are better off using it. But if you are convinced something else is better, I won't go to the mat on it. The point is not the savings vehicle. The point is the dollars. All those dollars that must be saved to have enough.

But for folks like me who just want something easy, uncomplicated, automated, and with a nice little tax advantage, the 529 is where it's at.

But wait, there's more. You can give this 529 account number to lots of people in the family, and say, "Hey, stop buying us plastic things that will be in the trash in six minutes. Please, give my kids the gift of college." And they might actually take you up on it, especially if you time the ask for that moment right after little Mikey climbs in Grandpa's lap and tells him he loves him.

Each state has a 529 plan, and that's where you should start, particularly if you live in a state that has a state income tax. Often, if you sign up for the state's 529 plan, then there will be a small state tax deduction on contributions. Otherwise, a 529 works like a Roth. You put money in after tax, grow the money in investments, and then when you take the money out to pay for college expenses you pay no income or capital gains tax.

Hence why you should run, not walk, to your computer when the social security number arrives. Because these suckers work like a Roth, you do not want to delay funding them. The earlier you can fund them, the more time the money can grow in *riskier* investments. In other words, the earlier you start, the harder investing can work for you. If you open one of these when your kid is in middle school, it's a little too late to get the benefit. By then you can't afford as much risk and you'll be invested in more bonds than stocks. With less ability to grow, it's just not as exciting at that point. (Remember our compound interest chart at the beginning of the book?) Whatever amount you can contribute early, do it!

529s typically have a target date fund available; remember those? They are age-based options, and you can choose how aggressive you want the fund to be. But, regardless of what you choose, you get to set it and forget it.

I include 529s in the section on savings accounts rather than Pay Yourself First, because college savings, while great and responsible, are not going to benefit you or your retirement. A lot of parents I have met with have 529s and no retirement. That just doesn't make sense. Put your oxygen mask on first. Trust me, junior can borrow for college. You cannot borrow for retirement. You'll end up burdening your child more if you can't take care of yourself in later years.

College is, in the end, an expense, and a *very* lumpy one at that. Once you decide how much you can afford to save for college, then you set up the 529 and create an automated savings deposit drafted from your main checking account. Hey, by the way, for help in figuring out how much to save for college, mosey on over to a great college calculator I use with folks: tools.finra.org/college_savings. I recommend a few minutes of deep breathing first.

Parents of young kids, you have not missed the savings boat. We love the windfall that comes with the pay raise from not paying for daycare anymore, assuming you are not doing private school. I remember that day we gleefully dropped our kid off for his first day of pre-K at public school. We got 800 $1 bills, dumped them out on our living room floor, and then swam around in them.

Yeah, not exactly.

We actually did two responsible things that I just have to recommend here—the ultimate buzz kill for anyone chomping at the bit for a home remodel or new car with thanks to the newly found windfall.

First, catch up on college savings. We increased our monthly transfer when we got our first pay raise.

Second, we started saving for summer. Oh my goodness, the camps, the babysitters, and the activities. When you add it up, it could (and likely will) cost thousands. Trust me, it's hard enough juggling the punishing schedule of summer. You don't want the added stress of a money shortage on top of it.

There are other kid things that are similar to summer and hit the budget hard. Expensive dance schools or uniform costs or seasonal activities with one-time fees are tough. Back-to-school shopping for some folks can be hard. Anticipate these tough times by thinking through the year to plan when and how much they hit. Then, you guessed it, start a savings account. Call it "kids" or "lil stinkers" for some fun. If you pay for any of these activities on a monthly basis or less often, then it should not be treated in the savings account section. That would be handled in the next section as a regular bill to keep your life as simple as possible.

☑ **ACTION 1:** Open a 529 plan or other savings vehicle. Navigate the tension between what your college savings goal is and what you can actually afford to save on a monthly basis, then set up an automated savings contribution to the savings plan.

☑ **ACTION 2:** Open a savings account for kid activities if you have seasonal activities that can derail your budget. Add up the cost of all the activities and camps and then divide by 12. That is the monthly auto transfer from your main checking account to your "kid" account.

Save for Dreams/Future Expenses

Pay Yourself First

***** TAXES & DEDUCTIONS *****

SAVE FOR EMERGENCIES

**SAVE FOR DREAMS,
FUTURE EXPENSES**

Action item

Establish a variety of savings accounts into which certain pre-determined amounts of money will be automatically transferred, allowing you to pay for unexpected/dream expenses when they arise.

Making it Work

Now, to put these beautiful savings accounts into action. What I want you to do is really simple. You can download the guide at ButFirstSave10.com.

1. Pick the spending items in your life that are large/lumpy and list them in Step 2.

2. Estimate how much they will cost per year and write that amount down next to each item.

3. Divide the annual number by 12 to get the cost on a monthly basis.

Pause here: Record your monthly savings on the worksheet, but we have to now do the rest of the math on bills and lifestyle to make sure these are affordable.

Then, we execute the rest:

4. Open the accounts with your bank. (Or in the case of emergency fund, HSA, or 529, at different institutions.)

5. Set up automatic transfers with your bank in the amounts you need to save each month from your master checking account to each savings account.

6. When it is time to spend, the money is there. Transfer it back into your master checking account and make your purchase. (We will talk about another option to use a credit card and reimburse yourself with the savings accounts, as well.)

This is budgeting at its simplest. Instead of one large savings account to pool everything together, you get to have razor sharp savings for the myriad things that happen through the year that are tough to plan for.

Why so many savings accounts? Well, we all know that "rob Peter to pay Paul" pitfall. If we have one savings account for everything, how will we know what's allocated for clothes, home repairs, or the oil change this month? It would be nearly impossible to keep a tally of it. There are apps that can do this, but they require you to enter data on deposits and withdrawals—again, unnecessary work.

The answer is separate savings accounts. Turns out you can have a lot of them. As I mentioned above, I have 8, including the 529. And they don't cost me anything. In fact, the bank actually pays me via interest to have them. (It's not much, but still, free money!) It's a magical windfall for successful budgeting.

If you've gone to one of the Save10 events, I assume you're already using this worksheet. If you are young and just out of college, you may have found that four of the savings accounts made sense, like emergency fund, vacation, car, and gifts. You gleefully pictured $75 going into your emergency fund that you renamed "freedom fund." In fact, you probably took me up on my advice to open that account at a different bank altogether. Your company has a partnership with a credit union, and you signed up for an account at work, asking HR to send the $75 every month right out of your paycheck. This account is so important to you, and you became determined not to rob it.

That leaves three savings accounts to set up at your bank for taking an annual vacation, saving for car repairs and your next car, and buying gifts. You have the amounts imagined, but first you need to do the rest of the process to make sure those amounts will work.

If you are a homeowner with kids, I would guess all of the savings accounts probably made sense. Maybe more! I just laid out the most common accounts that our clients typically open. Go to your worksheet now and total up how much money you will ideally have transferring out of your master checking account and into each of those accounts.

This cash management system is an iterative process, meaning now we have to go through the rest of the system to see if we can afford these amazing accounts. If there is enough left over for our bills and discretionary spending (Steps 3 and 4), then this is the easiest system ever. For most people, that is not the case.

If there is *not* enough money left over, then you will be left with a decision. Where do you cut? We will get to that later, but start thinking about ways you can reduce spending or bills to make funding these savings accounts work. And, spoiler alert, happiness lies in the savings buckets. Please, please, please try not to cut there if possible.

The reason I love these accounts is that you get to avoid the common plague of being operationally poor, meaning your budget works to pay the bills and buy groceries. It just breaks down and makes you poorer when the inevitable, lumpy, one-time expenses hit, like a last-minute weekend trip with the girls or a tire that blows out and ends up on a credit card. No more! Not with your savings accounts. When those problems arise, you get the familiar wave of nausea at the sight of the medical bill or your share of the group's baby shower you just threw. But then, in a panic you open your banking app and see the list of your savings accounts. You get to the health account, and, "phew" there is $1,000, more than enough to cover the $300 visit to the specialist. The $200 for the baby shower? No sweat. You have $300 in the gift account.

If you see the vision, go ahead and set up your accounts. Once you finish the next two steps of the cash management system and make sure you can afford those savings transfers, the following step is to set up the auto transfers to fund them. The final step is to learn how to spend out of the savings accounts. You can spend in one of two ways. First, you can use a credit card for them. I know, I know. How crazy after all the sickness we see with credit cards that I am now going to recommend them! But, truly, this can work well. Sure, you can spend on a credit card, but you also now know what your *exact* budget is for whatever you are buying. See a shirt at your favorite boutique? Trust me, you aren't whipping out the credit card without first looking at your banking app to see if you have money in your clothing savings account to buy that shirt. Is it time for new tires? Open up your bank app. Is the money there? Great, go ahead and buy the tires on your credit card. Then reimburse yourself from savings. You will pull the money from your "car" savings account to your main checking account. That main checking account pays the credit card.

Otherwise, if you have had bad experiences with credit cards or are just against them, you can use your master checking account to spend on these items. This is especially helpful for people who have no flexibility or margin in their budget. Let's call it precision budgeting. You go to buy that shirt at the boutique and, at the point of sale, instantly transfer the money from your savings account to your checking account, then swipe the debit card from your master checking account to purchase.

The brilliance of this cash flow system is in its automated nature and how little work has to be done once it is set up. Truly, the only "work" involved is reconciling your savings account at the end of the month. You set up this system to equal zero (we will get to that by the end). Therefore, if you spend money allocated in a savings account and don't reimburse yourself from that savings account, then obviously you will overdraw the account. The system has your motivations aligned so well that unless you unwind the budget, you are highly incentivized to do what needs to be done.

In other words, if you spend money related to travel or gifts or car repairs from a credit card, when it comes time to pay your credit card in full at the end of the month, you will not have the money to pay the full balance. You *have* to go through your credit card and add up how much you spend on every savings category and then transfer that amount to your master checking account. Then, just the right amount of money will be available to pay off the credit card in full.

If you are choosing not to use a credit card, rather just spending on those expense items directly out of your master checking account, you will run out of money before the end of the month if you don't pull over the money from savings into your master checking account. Before making a big purchase like airline tickets or buying that shirt, those who opt to use a debit card should make a quick transfer from savings to master checking account at the point of purchase. The clerk says that will be $50, and you quickly move the money from your clothing account to the master checking account. Then, you confidently swipe your debit card for that amount.

You might think this is cumbersome, but remember that these are rare and lumpy expenses. Let's take the shirt example. If you shop for shirts, jeans, and other clothes every month, then you shouldn't even have a clothing savings account. Clothing for you is a common monthly discretionary purchase and belongs in Step 4. I shop for clothes twice a year. My system is to set a budget for what I can spend by moving that budget amount over. This last January it was $400. Before I went to the mall, I moved $400 to my checking account and then used my debit card to spend that amount. But I could have moved the funds each time I was checking out at the registers of various stores when I found out how much the purchase cost. Do what works for you.

Remember, these expenses by their very nature don't happen often. Therefore, the process of transferring funds at the time of purchase is not a heavy lift.

The reason other budgeting systems fail is that they require you to find motivation that isn't necessary and therefore won't always be there. For instance, a budgeting app that requires you to categorize expenses is asking you to take an extra step to do something superfluous, or "extra." Sure, it would be nice to know what you have budgeted for an item and if you are on track. But it is not necessary. You can still purchase things. You can still overspend. The extra work to log into the app and categorize your 15 expenses for the day when life gets busy becomes less and less of a priority. You miss one day, then two days, then a month, and it's over.

But here's the beauty of this system. You can't overspend. The auto transfers to fund the budgets get made automatically. You need the money. But then you have to get it. You *have* to get it only from where there is money. If you want to buy something, but your banking app says the money is not there, then you simply can't buy it. You will end up overdrawing the account if you do.

You are using this budget for making future decisions. You are not making the decision, then looking at the budget to reflect on *past* decisions. I call that forensic budgeting, and, folks, it not only *doesn't work*, it fuels that judgement and self-loathing that we don't need any more help with.

Also, with this system you have to take the 5 to 10 minutes to reconcile your budget at the end of the month or you will overdraw your account when you go to pay your credit card balance to zero (if you are using one). Let's say you use the credit card to pay for items that will ultimately be paid out of your savings accounts. At the end of the month, you will open up the credit card and then get out a spreadsheet or a piece of paper. Simply go through it, and add up all clothing-related items on the credit card. Then, transfer the sum total spent on that category to your master checking account. Do the same for every single expense (except bills—we will get to those). Anything on your credit card that is not a bill needs to be assigned to one of your savings accounts and reimbursed to your checking account at the end of the month. Then, voilà! You can pay your credit card bill, knowing the money is safely in the checking account. We offer a simple Excel tool available for download at ButFirstSave10.com to help you do this end-of-the-month calculation.

For precision budgeting, or my budget ninjas, you would not reconcile at the end of the month. Instead, when it is time to buy something associated with your savings accounts, pull the money over from your savings account to your master checking account, and then write the check or swipe the debit card. This is real-time budgeting at its most elemental, beautiful level. Forget the credit cards and any points or offers they might be giving up. Budget ninjas sleep so well at night. No end-of-month surprises for them.

2. Save for Future Expenses
Automate Savings

Set up savings accounts earmarked for emergency fund and other expenses (i.e. home repairs, new car, vacation, gifts, etc.)

Emergency: $_____ / month

_____ : $ _____   _____ : $ _____

_____ : $ _____   _____ : $ _____

_____ : $ _____   _____ : $ _____

_____ : $ _____   _____ : $ _____

_____ : $ _____   _____ : $ _____

Savings Total = $ _____ / month

(Net Pay) - (Savings Total) = $ _____   (A)

STEP 3: PAY YOUR BILLS

Just pay 'em. That's the answer to Step 3. But while we're here, I want to philosophize a bit. I recently learned sage wisdom that Sharon Johe, a rad rockstar female attorney in Winston-Salem, North Carolina, has taught her grandkids. When she asks them the secret to a happy life, they answer what she has repeated to them time and again, "low, fixed overhead."

So maybe let's not just pay 'em. Let's take a little time and go one by one to eliminate our bills, reduce them, and if we can't do anything about them, at least levelize them (make them the same each month).

We consider all overhead, or regular bills, to be essentially, and in some cases literally, unchanging. This is important. When it comes to money, our brains get tired. They get tired of making decisions, especially. Decision fatigue is a real thing. If you find yourself making a decision on paying your rent, meaning trying to find the money to pay it, tracking down a checkbook, or opening an app to Venmo it, then you just wasted precious brain power. Your rent is not a decision. You live in a place and contractually agree to pay the same amount every month. Why would you spend any time thinking, considering, planning, or executing that rent payment?

Bills represent a part of your budget that will not have to be watched unless you do something to change them. These are the bills you must pay to live where you live. Society tells us that we will be so much happier the greater amount it costs us to live—larger homes, more expensive cars, better clothes, etc.—but research reveals, and I believe, that our guts tell us otherwise.

Bills, to us, can be rent payments, mortgage payments, car payments, utilities, cable, cell phones, gym memberships, skin care memberships, etc. They are also where we house minimum payments on debt.

The secret of this cash management system is that it's the only one that lets us come face-to-face with the painful tradeoffs we make, particularly when we add to our bills, or overhead. Because when you add bills, you must take away money from something else. With this bigger home, are we trading an extra date night with our spouse? Adding five years to our working lives? Sentencing ourselves to jobs we can't leave if they no longer make us happy?

I was recently speaking to a friend who worried about the long-term prospects of her job. She was so talented, customers loved her, but there was no room for material advancement. One day she got a small promotion that came with a pay raise. She bought a car the next week with a monthly payment larger than the pay raise. Her exact words were, "Well, I guess I have to love my job now. I can't go anywhere."

There is no doubt that in that moment, she wanted that car and believed (and maybe still believes) that the car was worth the tradeoff of freedom. I find myself wondering if she had created a plan for her life and career whether she might not have made the same decision.

What is your belief system? Is there any purchase you could make that would be worth the cost of your freedom to leave a job or a toxic relationship? I work with so many young people directly out of college, and they seem to get it. They say "no", and they seem totally willing to buck the trends of so many payments that become high fixed overhead. The ones that struggle are the ones that have already made the decisions, already bought the car or house or furniture that was financed with monthly payments. Remember, it's much harder to back down a lifestyle than to ramp one up.

Reduce or Eliminate Bills

I remember when I used to spend everything I made that the idea of cutting a small, recurring bill of, say, $5 per month was not worth my time. I recall thinking, *Why bother? It all gets spent, anyway.* Have you ever felt that or said something similar to yourself? *If I eliminate $5, probably it would be replaced by $10.* Or, *Why eliminate $5? That wouldn't make a dent in my budget.* You are hardly alone in this thinking. Without a system for money, a bunch of money flows in, and then by the end of the month, it all flows out.

When I implemented this system, I suddenly became greedy for that $5. I think you will experience that as well, especially once you get through Step 4. That $5 that could direct transfer into my vacation fund, my retirement account, or into my weekly spending budget. (We are getting there next—don't worry.) Over four years, that $5 per month becomes the cost of a plane ticket. Let's say you found that $5 and increased your retirement savings by that amount. Assuming a 6% rate of return, that $5 per month becomes over $4,700 over 30 years. The point is, that $5 will be captured, reallocated, and loved. Then, if you are like me, when you trust the process, you become hungry for more. How much can you negotiate down the car insurance? That cell phone bill crept up from $100 to $150 over the last two years—what can I do to get it back down to $100?

This system will help you think of your overhead in a different light. Suddenly your bills are a series of tradeoffs. The tradeoff is happiness, security, and freedom. This isn't to say all bills are bad. I have bills that do bring happiness and convenience. I love the home we own and gladly pay our property tax and insurance bill to remain here. I am comfortable with an internet connection and the Netflix and Sling services we pay for. But I am constantly asking the question if they still bring happiness and utility. I used to have a gym membership that was expensive, and when life got more hectic with my company ramping up, speaking engagements at odd times, and my kids getting older with more activities, I just couldn't go to the classes at the times they offered. My old self would have continued to allow that $120 per month auto draft for at least 6 months before making that decision. My new self cancels it the very next month since the usage wasn't paying off and I wasn't deriving happiness from it.

Please don't be afraid of the challenge. Ultimately, we want to find joy and contentment in our lives, and after my own experience with the cash management system and being on the path with hundreds of clients, I am convinced that almost uniformly, we can find incremental happiness by reducing our dollars that we pay in bills and diverting them to our savings and/or dream accounts.

Pay Your Bills

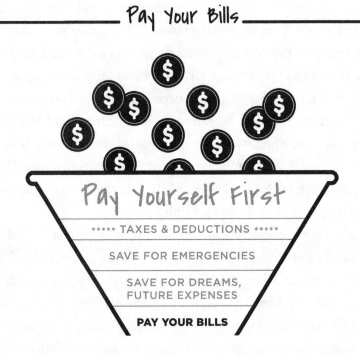

Pay Yourself First

***** TAXES & DEDUCTIONS *****

SAVE FOR EMERGENCIES

SAVE FOR DREAMS,
FUTURE EXPENSES

PAY YOUR BILLS

Action item
Eliminate, reduce, and levelize your fixed expenses.
Auto-pay them from your master checking account each month.

---

3. Pay Fixed Expenses

Automate payments for fixed expenses, (i.e. rent/mortgage, utilities, cell phone, internet, minimum payments for credit cards & other debt)

_____ : $ _____ /month

_____ : $ _____   _____ : $ _____

_____ : $ _____   _____ : $ _____

_____ : $ _____   _____ : $ _____

_____ : $ _____   _____ : $ _____

_____ : $ _____   _____ : $ _____

_____ : $ _____   _____ : $ _____

Total = $ _____ / month

(A) - (Fixed Expenses) = $ _____ (B)

Paying bills is the simplest step in our cash flow system and it is meant to save you time.

To begin, in Step 3, please fully account for your bills. Do not overlook anything, not even that $2.99 for expanded Cloud storage. I want you to spend a few hours and pull every statement from every checking account or credit card you have. Go through the last three months, at least, and make sure you have captured every bill or recurring payment. Feel free to download our bills expense review at ButFirstSave10.com to complete this step. Many of the bills listed will be zero, but the list will make sure that you haven't overlooked anything.

Got them down? Ok, now add them up and write the total in Step 3, factoring them into your formula.

Handling bills in the cash flow system is simple. Your goal is to automate them by putting as many on auto pay as possible. The philosophy of bills is that they should not take up brain space. Use this time to consider them, vet them, confirm them, and then automate them. Your brain actually has limited capacity for making hard decisions. It gets tired! Do you want to spend time physically receiving bills and scheduling online checks or credit card payments to them, when you know you are paying them, regardless? No! Please, save your brain power for Step 4, where you *are* making decisions on a daily basis. You want those to be the daily decisions.

As mentioned, use this opportunity to do whatever you can to eliminate or mitigate bills. We all have that bill about which we know we can do better. Have you shopped your car insurance lately to get a better deal? Do you have an app that is debiting your account each month, even though you don't use it anymore? Get rid of it! I have had clients discuss the headache of dropping a $7 per month subscription to a fitness website, but imagine saving saving $84 per year. Imagine eliminated a $10 per month debit ($120), a $14 per month debit ($168), and an extra channel on TV that you never watch for $7.50 per month ($90). You've just gotten rid of four expenses for items or services that you no longer want, and you have saved $462 per year. And let me add, it is not uncommon for people to look at their credit card statements or bank accounts and see recurring debits that they *do not recognize* and have no idea where the money is going or for what. Now is the time that you can deal with that debit, eliminate it, and put it to much better use.

As you will see when you take this journey, you will have every incentive to find $5. The system will protect you from surprises, put your dreams on a financial pedestal, and send what's left to paying bills and lifestyle preferences. My clients who test drive this program begin to realize that every dollar of overhead they can reduce or eliminate can go directly into accounts that will give them greater satisfaction, happiness, and peace of mind.

Not convinced? Ironically, overhead is the one area of spending in which it is very difficult to find happiness. Houses cross Step 2 and Step 3. In Step 2, we decide how much to save for a down payment or how much to save into a repair reserve or property tax/insurance reserve if the house is paid off. In Step 3, we decide if we want a mortgage payment. A mortgage payment is the breaker of happiness in my opinion. I am not averse to a mortgage. I am averse to a mortgage that squeezes out everything else. Right now, banks will approve loans that would leave the borrower with a payment (including insurance and taxes) that represents 28% (often much more than that) of gross monthly pay. So, let's do back-of-the-envelope math here. You pay yourself first 10%, pay taxes up to a rate of 30%, and pay health and other paycheck benefits of 5%. This leaves only 55% left to spend on everything else, from student loans to cars to food to gas to childcare to college savings to travel. Oh, and what about the home repair reserve to maintain that house? Trust me, the math doesn't add up.

So why do people do it? I believe it is because they don't do this simple math. Instead, they make the isolated decision: Should we buy the house or not? They are not making the trade-off calculation: What are we giving up by buying this house? They might not realize that homes can be rented as an option, instead thinking that the trade-off is rent an apartment or buy a home.

I feel a lot of compassion for people making a home purchase decision. Houses offer the promise of social acceptance, grand parties full of laughing people, and small children joyfully (and quietly?) contenting themselves in each of their private rooms. But what is the reality? Houses don't bring friends. Parties are a brief flash in the many moments of living under one roof. Children will always prefer to be as close as possible to you in their younger years. You will want to be physically closer to them in their older years. And there's the dreaded adolescence when no one wants to be with anyone!

My observation in financial planning is that of all the purchases people strive for, homes are the dream killers. I have tried talking clients out of the notion of "stretching" into a mortgage payment. Those who move forward with it find life more challenging than before. They can't easily pay for an occasional dinner out. They may have to reduce how much they are saving for retirement. They must continually put off saving for the kids' college educations. Or, even more scary for young people starting careers, that home can prevent them from taking risks on new jobs or moving for opportunities. If you find yourself using the word "stretch" when describing a potential mortgage, realize there is no "stretching" when it comes to money. There is only substitution, and in my experience, the tradeoffs are far too expensive.

On the flipside, I have seen clients get into houses that are less expensive than what lenders would have approved for them. Many of my doctor clients are trending into much smaller houses than their numbers would support. Instead, as we do their planning, they will take those thousands in savings every year and prioritize them into larger/more luxurious vacations or extra savings to retire early.

While it is not common, I have seen people intentionally downsize homes to pursue dreams, mostly dreams of going back to school or starting a new business. They have been able to face down the intense social pressure to own increasingly larger homes because they so clearly see a vision of the life they want. They want to be their own bosses, generate money for themselves—not just the company they work for—or invest in a new area of employment that would bring them daily joy. I don't expect someone reading this book to be so inspired that they sell their home and move into a small apartment in order to pursue a dream. But be aware that using this cash management system will probably result in continuous considerations of similar alternatives.

Back to Olivia, the version of herself before she started managing her money. At any given point, her bank account may show that she has $2,000 or $200. Money simply comes and goes with such speed and irregularity that trade-offs are nearly impossible to consider because she can't even see what the trade-offs are. Even the notion of cutting expenses and gaining $300 per month may seem fruitless. But let's say she started this cash flow system and has $1,000 of her money "disappearing" for retirement, dreams, emergencies, and the "known unknowns." This leaves $1,400 per month. Is she going to get that apartment for $1,200 per month? No, because she can pinpoint the trade-offs—mostly the ones that deal in happiness.

Many of our clients stay in the home they started in. They become deeply aware of the trade-offs and continuously validate their home. But some have looked hard at their mortgage payments and weighed the opportunity costs of those payments. They've concluded that those costs were simply too high to justify the loss of what they valued and wanted.

Vehicles, also like homes, straddle Steps 2 and 3. If you save ahead for a car, then you end up buying less car, and a trend I have noted is the downsizing of vehicles and buying in cash. Car payments are like mortgages, and as a bill they go in Step 3. It is much easier to buy more car when financing one with a car payment. We have had many clients say farewell to luxury vehicles. My husband and I are in that group. Many millennial couples are opting for one-car, one-Uber families, which can be a very cost-effective way of handling transportation, especially for people who work in proximate parts of town or who live near their jobs. This may even reflect society pivoting to reevaluate the notion of car ownership. Cars and homes and the payments that come with them can be status symbols and can make people feel they can more easily manufacture a sense of being successful, even if the reality doesn't match the sense. But the sacrifices to future self are simply too high. As Dr. James M. Dahle, blogger and author of The White Coat

Investor, so perfectly states, "It is far easier to be young and poor than to be old and poor."[42]

Below is an exercise to help you find any overhead that you can eliminate now but also a more reflective exercise to start you on the path of considering trade-offs of your overhead against your values. As you move forward with this system, you will start naturally wanting more resources to go into your long-term savings or dream savings account. I recommend you constantly reevaluate your overhead until you can get it as lean as possible.

Easy cuts: Now that you have your list of bills, I want you to go through and cut anything you simply haven't gotten around to cutting. Take action. Call the company. Wait on hold. Do what you need to do to persevere and get those out of your budget. Investigate your credit card and checking accounts, and look for any expenses, subscriptions, websites or apps you are currently paying for that you no longer use. Do you pay insurance on something you don't need? On my last cell phone, I was paying insurance every month of $14; when it broke and it was time to make good on the insurance, the deductible I had to pay was the cost of replacing the phone. Lesson learned to drop the insurance much earlier. Have you built a savings cushion for your car? Look at your auto insurance policy, and see if you have a low deductible. This means if you have a collision or have damage to your car you only pay $100 or $250 before insurance then pays the rest. A low deductible is an expensive premium because it means that you are paying to have the insurance company take the lion's share of the responsibility. You could consider increasing that deductible, save on premiums every month, and perhaps save that extra money into a vehicle fund for vehicle repairs or a future vehicle.

The great thing about easy cuts is that this is the perfect time to recapture those expenses. Before, you may have thought, "What's the point? It's just $14." Now you have a good and important use for that $14. Over the course of a year that $14 is one and a half months' contributions to an emergency fund in the example above.

Aspirational cuts: I might also call these the "Let's Be Real" cuts. Look through the rest of the list. Like me, you pay $120 per month for the gym membership. You rarely go. You need to go. Going will make you healthier. You maintain the membership to remind you to go. But let's be real, you are not going. So, discontinue the membership and of course you can pick it back up when you are in a phase of your life where it is practical. Maybe you even cut it to find that there's a special offer down the line when you need it again or join one of those $10 or $20 gyms that have the same equipment as the $120 gym.

Think through any other expenses or services that maybe you don't use or don't need. Are there any beauty services that could be cut or done less expensively? I am in love with pedicures and manicures, but when I started this system, I discovered that $40 per month probably had a better home. Now those "manis" and "pedis" are something special I only do with friends. Many find that they can do just as good a job at home with a kit.

As painful as this suggestion is for many, think about housekeeping and lawn service. For people doing this system just to have a better sense of control over money, firing the housekeeper may be off the table. For people who have a goal they clearly see—getting out of debt, going on vacation, saving for retirement—maybe this is an experiment worth trying.

I have a physician client at the pinnacle of his career who to this day still mows his own yard. He could definitely afford a lawn service. I have even suggested it, but he insists that this is an enjoyable activity for him. Remember, prepare to be surprised in this process. Maybe just experiment with these cuts to see if they are neutral or less painful than anticipated. You might even find them to be life enhancing.

Painful cuts: I reserve painful cuts for those in desperate situations. Often this includes crushing student loan debt or credit card debt, or living paycheck to paycheck. Every single monthly bill must be on the table for reconsideration. Start with the most obvious bill, which is the home (rent or mortgage). As I mentioned before, the home is typically the biggest burden, but is the one item I find people reluctant to change (unless it is to buy bigger). In actuality, those clients who are willing to downsize or sell their house in favor of renting did not regret it. In fact, one client shared an anecdote that downsizing gave her freedom from financial worry and caused her to delight in her kitchen's cheap laminate backsplash.

Remember, this is all an experiment. If you downsize your home and are completely miserable, then buy a bigger one. Go back to the way things were before. (Spoiler alert—you probably won't do that.)

Go through the same process with all your major monthly items. Do you have a car payment? Can you downsize your car? I have more physician clients than I can count on two hands that pull up to work in old clunkers. Driving cars to mileage over 200,000 is apparently a rite of passage for millennials now. Join that hip new movement. Or you can become a one-car, one-Uber family. The cost savings on insurance, fuel, and repairs might make sense for you.

Let's assume that you have your bills where you want for now. The next step is to make them the same each month. This system relies on regularity of spending, and bills should be that way. No surprises. The only problem is that some of our bills are irregular and can set a budget back. Consider the fluctuations of your utility bills. Some months could be $300 and others $30. That makes budgeting very difficult. In these situations, we recommend that you put all utilities on levelized billing if the company offers it. For bills that come quarterly (like pest control), semi-annually (like car insurance or private school tuition) or annually (like term life insurance), you can set up another savings account to accrue savings for each of these bills. The point is, when the bill comes in, the money is already there, and you don't have to look under the sofa cushions (or rob emergency or savings accounts) to find spare change.

The decision to pay down debt as part of the cash flow management system happens logistically in Step 3. You know how much to pay on the debt, but can you automate this payment through an Automated Clearing House (ACH) payment or an auto bill pay? Especially if you are committing to pay greater than the minimum payment, then just the small act of automating that payment will mean you are less likely to stop or reduce that payment.

Finally, how do you pay your bills using this system? Logistically, your income (paycheck) flows into your master checking account, and bills are paid from that account. Bills can also be paid by credit card. Personally, I use the system and I use a credit card, putting all bills possible on that card. To name a few, I have my internet, cell phone bill, and Netflix paid on the credit card. Because the master checking account pays the credit card statement each month in full, in the end it all comes from the same account.

Our goal for Step 3 is to account carefully for bills, reduce them, then automate them. Every year, you should take a careful look and evaluate your bills for possible reductions.

Finally, as you adopt this system, it will be clearer over time that adding payments reduces happiness. Those car payments, higher rent payments that are just a little higher than the ones before, and buying that new mattress with nothing saved means payments that will add stress and reduce joy. It used to be that we talked about spending our money in small ways until it was gone as "nickle and diming" our money away. We now have payments to replace that. Never in time have there been more opportunities and pressures to payment your happiness away.

Go to your worksheet and fill in your bills. Remember, use a pencil—with an eraser.

STEP 4: SPEND THE REST

Step 4 could also be titled "how to save a marriage," "how to stay out of crushing credit card debt," or "finding the edge of your money." You get the point. It's dramatic.

Step 4 is not as much a step as a condition. The condition is that you get to spend what is left in your account. But, there is a trick to spending the rest.

This step is so crazy simple and fantastic as a single person. You have a spending amount, you are the only one spending, you know how to get from Monday to Sunday on that amount.

For couples, this becomes a little more like a tango.

As I write this, I am out of money. Our pantry is limited. We had enough for a grand breakfast and sandwiches for lunch, but dinner was a little more difficult. The choices were beans and rice, or a spoonful of peanut butter, all around. While the kids probably would have preferred the latter, we went with the former, and it was the scaled down version—no meat, no tomatoes, no yuca, no avocado to top it off. We literally had run out of money. My husband prepared it the best he could, and to our surprise, all three kids wolfed it down.

After dinner, my husband dressed for his soccer game. As he called out, "See you at the field," it dawned on me: my gas light had come on earlier that day. Usually Jorge goes early to warm up, and I take the kids later, but if we wanted to go to the game today, we had to go together. There was no way I could get there and back without refueling. A frantic chase of three kids to get them ready was not exactly what I would sign up for on a Sunday afternoon, but that's what we did. I should reveal that there was a moment of insanity when I eyed my five-year-old's allowance on the counter. Luckily, that passed quickly. A mad dash ensued. The kids love going to the fields, and I wasn't going to let my spending earlier in the week impact their fun. So, I tore through the house collecting shoes, socks, t-shirts and shorts, filling water bottles, and chasing down soccer balls. We rode to the field together. We laughed on the way. My five-year-old rolled down the window. The baby sang. The three-year-old told us a story. And it was more fun. The whole family got to go this time. The day was a victory of the system.

Or you may think—um, it sounds like you were completely irresponsible? You ran out of money!

The truth was that we were far from spending our last dollar. We had probably a dozen different levers I could have pulled (and in my last life *would* have pulled). We had two credit cards with a combined limit of $30,000. We had a large emergency fund. We had a master checking account with several thousand in it. We had savings accounts earmarked for clothing, travel, health, home, and vehicle that all contain money. I could have easily transferred enough money to fill my tank and buy us dinner, but I didn't. This system has saved me. It has saved our family. It has made us creative. It has gotten us out of ruts. It has opened new ways of having fun—more fun—than we ever had before.

How to Spend the Rest

Intrigued? Here's how you spend the rest. Your monthly take home pay minus your savings account transfers minus your monthly bills equals how much you can spend.

How to Spend the Rest

Pay Yourself First

***** TAXES & DEDUCTIONS *****

SAVE FOR EMERGENCIES

SAVE FOR DREAMS,
FUTURE EXPENSES

PAY YOUR BILLS

**SPEND
THE REST**

Action item
Spend the rest of your money down to zero either monthly or weekly.
(Open a second checking acccount and use a debit card
to keep yourself on track.)

But it's not that easy. If we spent the rest out of our main checking account that has all the noise of the bills and timing of the auto transfers to our savings accounts, we could make some serious mistakes. There might be money in that account today, but it's gone tomorrow. We don't want to make a spending decision on money that's not really there. So, the first hack for "spend the rest" is a separate account where we can move the spending money and not get confused with bill or savings account money.

Most of us humans really stink at budgeting on a monthly basis. And I don't want you to stink at this. It turns out we can budget much better on a *weekly* basis. Our brains can know almost precisely over time how much money we ought to have to get us through the week by Wednesday, Friday, and, yes, on Sunday.

Go to your worksheet and make the calculation for "spend the rest." Multiply your monthly spending by 12 to get the amount on an annual basis, and then divide by 52 to get it on a weekly basis. Next, I want you to open a second checking account and then set up an auto transfer at your bank from your master checking account to your new spending account every Monday for your weekly amount.

This weekly amount is your "number." It is a number you will know, remember, obsess over all the time. It's the number that you will love in the weeks where you have leftover money to spend on fun stuff or to transfer to dream savings, or it's a number you will despise on the weeks when you run out of money by Saturday and are cleaning out the pantry to eat on Sunday. This number will become deeply personal to you, but you will gleefully honor it because for the first time in your life, this number represents your first taste of your own power to save, to find meaning in life with money, and to forever stop even the *possibility* of getting into credit card debt. This is radical self-care.

Can you feel that strength and awe coursing through your body? Let's make sure you understand how this works. Setting up your spending account is probably the trickiest piece of the cash flow system, and I want to make sure you get it right. To recap, your goal is to get your leftover money, the spend-the-rest money, from your monthly budget divided into weekly chunks. You will then have your bank auto transfer that weekly chunk every Monday from your main checking account into a checking account just devoted to spending. Your only effort on this spending account is to use a debit card and spend it to zero every week. Or, if it doesn't cramp your style that week, leave a little for another week and treat yourself to a bigger extra or pass it along to another account.

Now you have a weekly budget that funds your life. Most weeks it is more than enough—for our family, the weeks where we plan, don't eat out for lunch, and can avoid dry cleaning. I usually scoop out the leftover money at the end of the week and send it to our clothing or vacation account. But some weeks, we just spend too much early on, and it leaves us in a pickle. In a way, the weekends we run out of money are the most fun. In a past life, I lived in feast or famine. The feast was the beginning of the month when I had a lot of money in checking. The famine was the end of the month when nothing was left. And I really mean nothing. No levers to pull. That kind of nothing is stressful. The lever I would have to pull under those circumstances was using a credit card that sentenced me to a very stressful month, or months, down the road or maybe borrowing money from parents (a last resort).

In this cash flow system, we create an "edge" of the money. We experience how far the money can go. Without this system our cash flows, bill pays, debit cards, credit cards, and timing of income make it nearly impossible for us really to know what and where and when we hit the edge of our money, until it is gone or, oftentimes, overspent. We don't know we have overspent until we can't pay a bill that hit late in the month or we get a credit card statement with a balance that is higher than the amount of money in our checking account. In this new process, we can take what we make, remove the retirement savings, take out intra-year savings accruals, and take out the bill-paying money. This will bring you to the amount you really *can* afford to spend. From there, you can spend that amount to zero every week.

Do you notice something missing? Tracking. You have been waiting and bracing for it. Even though I told you at the beginning that you wouldn't have to do it, you just knew there would be some "but" or caveat that would require you to feel pain, shame, judgment, dread for spending money. It's that terrible part of the book where you have to commit precious minutes or hours to judging every expense that you spend on, every Starbucks coffee, every dinner out with friends; but no, you really don't. I can gleefully share the news that there is no "but." I don't care what you spend. And you don't have to either. Blasphemy, I know. But you've got your formula right there next to you, so let's recap. Are you paying yourself first? (Yes.) Are you saving for things you care about and for unknown disruptions? (Yes.) Are you paying all your bills? (Check.) So then why do you need to care a hoot about how you spend the rest? The answer is you don't. You just spend it, on whatever you want, until it's zero. Then Monday morning you start back over again with a pot of money to spend to zero.

I could have cheated in this process. And, trust me, if we had a serious emergency come up or something even slightly urgent that required me to fuel up my car, I would have done it. I would have pulled out that credit card in a heartbeat. But as a former spender who never could save before I cannot describe the delight in our retirement accounts. I cannot describe the feeling of knowing I have seven savings accounts that all have money in them earmarked for contingencies or true life-giving fun. I love the fact that I have $30,000 in credit card limits that I don't need. So, if it is Sunday, the last day of the week, and our living budget goes to zero, then we spend nothing. Happily, and gleefully, we spend nothing.

For couples embarking on this cash management system, this may be the harmonious joining of the spender and the saver, quite possibly the only time and place they will ever meet in peace. The spender gets to know the limit of what there is to spend. The saver gets the benefit of knowing that money is being saved and that there is money to spend without worry. They don't have to constantly squirrel away money and defer spending in fear that there probably won't be enough. They both get to know the edge of their money. This part of the system answers the question, how much money can I (we) spend?

How do you stay on this budget? Do you tediously write down your expenses each week? Do you track how much you spent on your groceries that week or latte runs to Starbucks? Nope. You just have your weekly spending money deposited into a second checking account that you or both you and your partner access through debit cards. You spend that account down to zero. Every week. It doesn't matter how much money you spend on any item. Just spend exactly what you have in that account, and everything will work.

How do you know you are on track through the week? You don't want to spend it all on Monday, right? Well, your bank has an app for your phone, and it keeps your balance updated real-time. So, your bank balance *is* your budget. And, again, you will get comfortable over time knowing just how much you should have every day of the week so as to not run out of money. Your budgeting will get *better* over time.

You will be saving for retirement. You will be taking vacations. You will be preparing to replace your roof. And now you will be using a simple-to-follow budget that is not burdensome time-wise to maintain. You and/or your spouse or partner will never have to question whether there is enough money for things. Your savings accounts will answer the question of how much you can afford for your next trip or to replace a broken appliance.

Your spending account will answer the question each day of whether you can go on that date, stock up at Costco, or pay the babysitter for a day outing. That account is where you can spend on "everything else." People always have a list: clothing, manicures, haircuts and colors, makeup and skincare, massages, and about a hundred other things. If the money is there, the answer is always "yes." It is everything else. You just can't spend more than what is in the account. Many clients ask what is an allowable purchase from this account? The absolute answer is anything that is not a bill and not accounted for by one of your savings accounts. But it still can be helpful to get a sense of what would need to come out of that account to determine if your weekly amount will fund everything it needs to. Here are some ideas of expenses that could be included.

(Remember, if you have a savings account for some of these things, then they would not be in the weekly cash flow.)

Dining In	Dining out	Fuel	Small Gifts
Hair and Beauty	Dry Cleaning	Miscellaneous	Clothing
Entertainment	Manicures/ Pedicures	Car Wash	Crafting Supplies and Gardening

But, will the account have enough money in it to cover all the expenses that could arise? The answer to that question will become undeniably clear. It will no longer be a guess or an opinion. Let's say you fund this account on Monday with $300 per week, but by Thursday you have $20 to get you through Sunday evening. Either the amount is not adequate, or you have knowingly spent down to $20, and you're good with that for the next four days. This is where you "feel" the effects of budgeting—and that heat is our motivator in this system instead of retrospective shame. If you conclude that $300 is not an adequate amount for your lifestyle, then you have to find the money. Look to your overhead first. Can you reduce or eliminate any expenses to provide the amount of weekly money you need? What I've found is that clients, after doing the math many times, estimate their expenses and then engage in a circular, repetitious process to balance out the overhead and dream accounts in order to make sure that the money they need is what is left.

Remember, the goal is to have a budget that isn't set up to fail. I try to get clients to have a realistic goal for their spending amount. I would rather see clients save a little less initially for retirement or emergency funds than they had aspired to, because I know that a strong cash management system used over a lifetime will result in much greater savings overall.

Some people who adopt this budget are so thrilled to have a cash flow management system that they are willing to face whatever the weekly amount is and make it work. (Unless it's like $20 a week—then you probably have to make some adjustments.) Some people want to make sure the weekly budget is realistic, and the best way to do that is to do a spending review.

Go through the last six months of spending, and quickly add up all the spending that would have had to happen in the weekly spending budget. Or, another way to approach it, add up all expenses that would not be paid out of savings accounts or expenses that will be captured as a bill. Based on the spending review, do you think your new weekly spending budget could work?

The funny reality is that this final account has psychological benefits that make it easier to save naturally. My clients almost uniformly report back that their weekly spending felt like more money than they needed. They had money left over each week. And studies support this by showing that spending money using a debit card (a balance that goes down) versus spending using a credit card (a balance that goes up) allows people to spend less money because they are more grounded in the reality of the numbers. In addition, having a steady weekly amount for spending regulates our habits and avoids the trap many of us fall into, burning through a lot at the first of the month when we feel richer and then having nothing later in the month. This effectively avoids the "feast or famine" that occurs when we don't have a plan. And remember, this is not a budget foisted upon you by someone else. Instead, this is a budget you have created for yourself after examining your personal values in quite a bit of depth.

The biggest expense that young people find hard to manage is a food budget—food used in a very liberal sense to include dining out and maybe the occasional night on the town. It can seem impossible to manage a food budget until using a system like the one I propose. I spend less right now on food with a family of five than my husband and I used to spend when it was just the two of us. The system makes us smarter about what foods to buy and how to make them last, more judicious about where and how often we eat out, and more conscientious of how expensive alcohol is. It used to be normal for us to order a margarita and a couple glasses of wine on a regular weekly dinner outing. Well, it took a weekly budget and to some extent opening a bar in 2016 for us to understand how expensive ordering alcohol with a meal really was. In Arkansas, hard liquor is taxed 28%. Let's do the math on the cocktail listed in the menu for $12. If you add taxes of $3.36 and a gratuity of 25%, or $3, then that $12 cocktail suddenly costs $18.36.

Is the answer to stop going to dinner? Honestly, it might be, but I would hope not. My husband and I used to go out to dinner all the time, but it was mainly because we didn't have a plan for dinner. How easy it was to just shrug our shoulders and hit a local restaurant. Now, eating out is a true experience. We plan ahead for it, get excited, and even dress up for the occasion. We go on a date, and while I will never stop cringing at the cost, we might spring for that second glass of wine. (Depending, of course, on what else we've already spent that week. Sometimes, I even plan ahead for the freedom of "splurging.")

Inevitably, you will find that some weeks you have money left over. If it is $25 or less, maybe you just carry it over to the next week. Some weeks are more expensive than others. Maybe you get gas every other week in your vehicle. Maybe you do bulk shopping once a month. There is a lot of irregularity that can happen in this account and it sometimes helps to have a small balance from low spending weeks to cushion high spending weeks.

A few years ago, I had a married couple in my office who were saving enough and had their retirement accounts shored up. But they struggled with the day-to-day spending. It caused a lot of discord between them. She had a lot of stress and anxiety about money and was always worried that they would run out. He was the opposite and believed that money was supposed to be enjoyed. They would inevitably end up with a credit card balance that couldn't be repaid, and she grew testier and testier as they went into credit card cycles. This was starting to weigh on their relationship. He wished she would lighten up. She wished he would take it seriously.

They learned the cash flow system and started implementing it. We worked out the logistics, and they got their weekly "number" of $420. By all means, this was a lean number for a family of five, but they got it working and reported back that the weekly was doable.

I met with them after a year and a half of being on the system. The first thing I noticed was how at ease they seemed, lacking the looks of stress and anxiety they'd worn before. I asked them how the system was going, and at first, they looked at me confused. My assumption was that maybe they had stopped? I clarified, "Are you still doing the weekly budget?" They laughed and said "yes." They still do the $420 per week, but the system was such a part of their life they didn't see it as a budgeting system anymore.

I asked why they had come to see me. There was a job change that they wanted to discuss. The question was whether to increase the weekly budget. After a long conversation about their hopes and dreams for the future, they said they wanted to put the extra money into retirement. Both of them dreamed of retiring early, and it would be possible with this extra savings. Importantly, he (the spender) said that the weekly amount was more than enough. They had figured out a lot of tricks to cut previous discretionary spending that was unnecessary, like expensive meals out just because they hadn't taken the time to meal plan. Every Sunday, they spend an hour or two figuring out what they eat for the week and do one shopping trip for it. In other words, he doesn't feel deprived.

She reported that she relaxed over time as she learned to trust the system. They could spend everything in that extra checking account, and she didn't have to worry anymore about overspending. The bills got paid, and they had money siphoned off for important savings accounts.

Having that weekly budget became routine and allowed them to refocus on their priorities and values. There is no doubt that in their former life, the raise would have just increased their lifestyle. Instead, they got to make a decision. Increasing their lifestyle would have been fine and appropriate. Afterall, their saving was a percentage. But the system allowed them to step back and reflect first, rather than letting inertia and the bank account lull them into spending more at the cost of the retirement they both wanted.

Gamification

One of the biggest breaks in personal finance have been in the success of gamification of money—literally, playing games, or tricks, to get you to save. This account will become that for you, as well. In my case and in the case of many clients, we make a game out of our spending account. My husband and I have agreed that I (as the spender in the marriage and the one who shops for the family more) could have the ultimate benefit of underspending. That's right, me. If we spend $100 less, it's mine.

We all have choices to spend less. I can make slow cooker meals for a whole week and end up saving us a lot of money on groceries and dining out that way. But that takes planning and effort. My incentive for that planning and effort is that I get to reap the benefits. So, if I want to get a massage one week or go on a fancy dinner date, then I make the effort to send us both to work with homemade lunches.

Marriage Saver

Even if you are single now, adopting this system can lay the groundwork for a healthy system if you get married. When we look at ways finances can cause divorce, most often the conflict I personally witness is when a spender is married to a saver. On one extreme, the saver kicks in and becomes militant about finances, dragging the unwitting spender along almost as a child in the financial relationship. Or, in the more common extreme, the spender prevails, and the saver bites her tongue to keep the marriage harmonious. But then the pain of the bad financial decisions, via credit card debt or undersaving, seeps into the marriage and causes toxic judgement to brew in the saver.

A friend recently told me a story about how money caused the downfall of her first marriage. She told me she never asked him questions about debt before marriage because in her family, to discuss money was taboo. It turned out that he had a mountain of credit card and student loan debt (hundreds of thousands of feet high), and didn't mind borrowing from her to pay it down. The problem is that the borrowing didn't come with the lifestyle changes she expected as a natural saver. Following the loan, he was dreamily clicking away at his computer, planning another expensive vacation on which he hoped she'd join him. His attitude was: "I'm not going to stop living because of debt." The marriage had difficulty as with every marriage, but the stress of the finances on top of it was too much, and it ended in divorce.

Imagine a different path for the successful union of the spender and saver that could start from the beginning—before there were problems. In fact, imagine if my friend in the course of planning finances got to learn the truth about his financial situation and outlook on life *before* they got married. Maybe she would not have married him. Or, if they did get married, they could have created and committed to a different financial arrangement and system from the beginning.

As I have alluded to many times, in my marriage I am the spender. My husband is the saver. But we are both operating in the same set of rules, namely our weekly lifestyle budget. We can take a trip—if the money's there. And we have a set amount to spend. No one's in charge. I am not sure if I could handle my husband criticizing my spending. The thought makes me shudder, and that is what is happening in so many marriages. Imagine managing money in a scenario where it's no longer personal. There is no more guessing about how much money is there, or what the "edge" is.

Savers have a difficult time spending, but I find that they relax into this cash flow system. When you pay yourself first and allocate to inter-mediate term savings accounts, then there is a license to spend in the now. It's ok to enjoy money. It's ok to see your spouse spending the money.

On a higher level, it is important to understand that the spending account is the only way to find the actual edge of your money. For the spender, the edge of money is the boundary beyond which you are living too much in the present without consideration of the future. For the saver, it is the line beyond which you are considering the future too much while the present is being ignored. It is clear that neither is practical, realistic, or healthy. But with an actual line that both people draw together, that financial line becomes a healthy one.

One more thing: I do not know from my own experience with hundreds of people if men or women tend to be spenders or savers. I find there is no real gender tendency for it. Couples will come in jokingly blaming the financial troubles on a woman's manicure or coffee habit only to realize it's the man's boat that is sinking their finances—a boat that would equal over 2,000 manicures or 22,000 cups of coffee. Sometimes, the big ticket items are the woman's, and the daily habits are the man's. The one-ticket answer of which gender tends to spend more just isn't there.

Luckily, unlike other systems, we only take a cursory look at the past. With a future-looking cash management system, couples quickly shift to what lies ahead, within their means.

Why a Debit Card for Step 4?

Many of my clients don't enjoy switching to a debit card for spending. In fact, some were so interested in points that they decided to create a system for mimicking the spending account with their credit card. The problem is, it just doesn't work as well.

A debit card offers a real-time balance on a weekly basis that goes down when you spend. The credit card takes a while to clear and offers a *monthly* balance that goes up when you spend.

The hack for the credit card was to know how much you should have in a given week of the month on the credit card. But the problem is that it's too easy to play games with it. Again, you are back to budgeting for the month. Only, before credit cards, when you are budgeting for the month, when the money is gone, it's gone. With credit cards, when the money is gone, you just get more money. And more money . . . and more money . . . and more money. More "sick" money. Then you are looking *backward* at how much you spent.

Another point to consider is all those credit card points are gamification for you to spend. Yes, there are people who use them brilliantly, but I think most people really end up getting tricked into spending money they wouldn't have spent otherwise. We tend to spend more on credit cards than debit cards. That, in turn, more than offsets the rewards as we discussed before.

Here's what I want you to do. Try the system with a debit card for a few months. Then take stock. If you are spending less money naturally, as my clients report, then you would be nuts to switch back to a credit card. Think about it—a credit card max can get you rewards worth 3% or 4%? But with this system, you might be looking at 20% to 30% reduction in spending. Plus, what would be the price of simplifying your life? Credit cards only make it more complicated.

Some people worry a lot that using a debit card exposes your account to being emptied if someone gets access to your card. Debit cards have really caught up in security to credit cards, and the industry is moving to chips with plans to move to even more secure modes of payment. But let's consider the fact that if your debit card account gets wiped, it's just your weekly spend. And remember the bank makes you whole if your account is compromised anyway.

How Should You Build Your Credit?

You need to build your credit score. Pronto. So how do you do it?

Well, remember there are places in this budget where using a credit card can work without the downfalls of credit cards. I use a credit card on any bill that will allow it and not charge a processing fee. I use it on some things related to dream savings, like booking flights and hotels for travel and insurance premiums where possible. None of those would put me at risk of "overspending." The only place I steer clear of credit cards is Step 4.

The goal is to build a profile in your credit report that shows you are creditworthy or have credit available to you. If you are able to obtain your first credit card, which might require a co-signer, then consider using a credit card for a small number of your monthly recurring bills. Think about subscriptions, cell phone bill, car insurance, etc. Then, put your credit card on auto pay for the full amount. Never ever miss a payment. Never ever carry a balance. Paying in full will build your credit. On-time payments will build your credit.

Next, over time, call up your credit card company and ask them to increase your credit limit. For instance, at first they might just give you a credit limit of $500. After 6 months, see if they will make that $1,000. You won't use that amount, but your credit score will improve over time as you demonstrate how much credit you have available but don't use.

Can't get a credit card? Don't have a co-signer? Consider finding a reputable bank in your area that can help you build credit using a secured credit card. Basically, you hand them cash, and they give you a credit card that allows you to borrow up to how much cash you have on deposit. Another approach is a credit builder loan where the community bank or credit union actually holds the money borrowed and you pay that back. I would look to this process if you don't have the upfront cash for a secured credit card.

Start there, and over time, as you pay your student loans, rent, and utilities, your credit score will build. I have seen a lot of young people who didn't make much money build their credit quickly by doing this. Where people get tripped up is when they make financial mistakes early on, missing payments or carrying large credit card balances as a percentage of their limits. They then must spend years recovering their credit.

As I said earlier on, financial pain does not have to be a rite of passage. You can avoid the financial mistakes with credit card debt that many people make in their early 20s. You can use them responsibly and make them benefit *you*.

4. Spend the Rest

THINK: All other expenses (i.e. gas, groceries, dining out, Netflix, clothes)

Option 1: Spend the rest (B) in your account down to zero each month.

Option 2: Go the extra mile! Open a second checking account
and spend weekly:

Take (B) x 12 = $_____ (C)

(C) ÷ 52 = $_____

Move this amount of money over each week into the second checking account and spend down to zero with a debit card.

THE BIG PICTURE

The system is simple to use over the long-term, but there are a few practical concepts to understand to make the system work. The first is auto-draft timing. You will have several auto drafts happening, and you will want to make sure the timing of the auto drafts will not cause you to overdraw your master checking account. In my case, I make sure we have a checking account "buffer" of a month's take-home pay so that the timing of bill payments and drafts will not cause the account to overdraw.

One way for you to achieve that is to ease into your savings accounts. Some clients who have razor thin budgets and no buffer end up funding savings accounts one month at a time. So, if you have a goal of funding six accounts, you would not have all of them funding for six months. For instance, you start with the emergency fund and direct the auto transfer to that account on month one. Then month two, you add an auto transfer to the vacation account, so now you are funding two accounts simultaneously. In month three you add the home repair account, and now you are funding three accounts at once.

By doing it gradually, you can also monitor your bills and make sure you haven't missed anything. You really don't want to inadvertently overdraft right out of the gate, causing you to incur fees, because you miscalculated or missed an expense.

The Big Picture

Pay Yourself First

***** TAXES & DEDUCTIONS *****

SAVE FOR EMERGENCIES

SAVE FOR DREAMS,
FUTURE EXPENSES

PAY YOUR BILLS

SPEND
THE REST

Action items

Call HR and have them contribute 10% of your gross pay to your retirement account. If you're self-employed, open a Roth IRA.

Open a savings account not linked to your main checking account. Auto transfer savings each month until you have 3–6 months of expenses saved.

Establish a variety of savings accounts into which certain pre-determined amounts of money will be automatically transferred, allowing you to pay for unexpected/dream expenses when they arise.

Eliminate, reduce, and levelize your fixed expenses.
Auto pay them from your master checking account each month.

Spend the rest of your money down to zero either monthly or weekly.
(Open a second checking acccount and use a debit card
to keep yourself on track.)

In addition, focus on *when* you get paid and then what would make sense for your savings auto drafts. For instance, if you are paid twice per month, consider letting the first paycheck cover your bills and your weekly spending auto drafts, and let the second paycheck cover your savings auto drafts.

When to use a credit card is pretty clear. We only want to use them in ways that would prevent us from falling victim to the psychological pull of spending via credit cards. Credit card companies know our behavior. They know that we will overvalue rewards so much that we will spend more money to capture increasing rewards. The most success in this system has happened when clients chose not to use a credit card—at all. The system works much more simply, and there is a lot less "budgeting" effort than when you must reconcile expenses on the credit card. I use a credit card in a very limited fashion, as do many of my clients. If you are needing to use a credit card to build credit, then there are relatively "safer" ways to do that in this budget. In my case we have the "UPromise" card from Barclay Bank that funds our kids' 529 plans. Each quarter we get $60 deposited into their accounts, and that makes me happy enough to use the card.

When it comes to your bill paying account, you can use a credit card for whatever bill will accept it, and I am finding a lot more companies will allow credit card drafts without fees. It makes sense that a credit card can be used on bills from school tuition to the cell phone bill to the internet bill. You have already made the decision to have them, and unless you decide to change or cancel them you don't need to waste brain power on them. The chance of overspending on these items does not exist. As for spending awareness, you will still know exactly what you spent on bills because you must reconcile your credit card each month, line by line.

Credit cards can be particularly handy when paying for emergencies, travel, or any expenses that should be paid from your savings accounts. Going on a trip? Sometimes it's even safer to use a credit card, so use it for all trip experiences from booking the flights and hotels to dining out. *But a small caution here.* Would you spend more than normal on a trip by using a credit card? Possibly? Probably! If this could be a problem, please consider alternatives. For our domestic trips, we do something cool. We decide on a "spending" budget for the week and then transfer that amount into our weekly spending account. It might be an additional $500 for going out to eat, passes to attractions, etc. We have a lot of fun but don't inadvertently overspend and have the travel hangover when we get back. The credit card is only used for the hotel, car, and flights.

The weekly spending account is the only off-limits account for the credit card. And if you think about it, it makes perfect sense. These are the daily spending decisions that control our ability to stay on track. A credit card that has an *increasing balance* doesn't nudge our brains to spend less. A debit card's *declining balance* more successfully gives us a nudge to spend less. Go with the debit card.

Reconciling Accounts Each Month

Each month, a few minutes of "work" are required to get your accounts in balance. Namely, you will have to reimburse yourself for spending you did in your master account or on a credit card that was linked to the savings accounts. Here's the thing: If you don't do it, you will run out of money. If you don't do it, you will have a credit card bill but no money in your checking account to pay it.

Unlike other budgeting programs where you *elect* to do the work, and therefore stop doing it, in this system you *have* to do it to survive financially. The incentive truly is built in.

At the end of each month, you have two accounts to reconcile: your master checking account and your credit card. Go line by line through the month's transactions. Any item that was a bill, you can essentially ignore, although I do recommend occasionally double checking that the amount is still correct. Otherwise, any other charge MUST be reimbursed from the appropriate savings account.

Clients who adopt this system usually find that their weekly spending budget is more than they need, even though we took their actual spending estimates from the prior year and made that their starting budget. I do not find this phenomenon a coincidence because of the behavioral studies around debit versus credit cards. The beauty of this cash flow management system is how little effort it takes to maintain long-term. Even better, there is a built-in incentive to spend those minutes. If you don't take the time to reconcile your accounts, you will not get to the money that's yours to spend.

I typically wait until the 1st or 2nd of each month to allow my credit card to settle out the expenses for the full previous month. I pull up an Excel spreadsheet and have seven columns representing each of my savings accounts: emergency, health, home repair, gifts, car repair, clothing, and travel. Then I go, line-by-line, through my master checking account and my credit card. If it is a bill, I ignore it (or occasionally review it for accuracy). If it is ANYTHING else, it must come from one of my savings accounts, which means I already have the money to pay it. As I mentioned before, you can pull up our reconciliation online at ButFirstSave10.com.

Let's say that in a particular month you paid for your hotel and experiences relating to a vacation. Include each of those expenses in the vacation column. Got new tires? Put that expense in the car column. Each item that is not a regular monthly bill needs to have a home. I feel the need to repeat that. Every single expense on your credit card or your master checking account that is not a bill must find a home. All expenses must be accounted for. If they are not, then the budget will not work. The result will be that you will overspend.

Precision is possible, but there have been times when I have been less than precise. Just this past December, I spent more on gifts and clothing than I had in those accounts, but the money must come from somewhere. I reluctantly took the money from travel and vowed to shuttle some of my weekly spending funds to travel to reimburse it. Years ago, when I first adopted the system, that situation would happen more frequently, but now, with experience, it happens less and less.

I have better awareness of my dream savings accounts and what is necessary to regulate my own spending to coincide with them.

Setting up the accounts is probably the easiest part. You (and your partner if you have one) need to map out your accounts first with the planning sheet at ButFirstSave10.com. If you can't set up savings accounts online through your bank, I recommend that you contact your bank ahead of time to start setting up the accounts you intend to fund. That way, the paperwork can be prepared for you before you arrive, and you can simply walk in and sign. Checking accounts cost money to maintain, but I do not worry about account fees that can be $7 to $10 per month for the two checking accounts. I can assure you that whatever I pay in fees is far less than what I spent on "who can remember" before the system.

Savings accounts are usually free. And your bank will pay interest on those accounts, although not much. If you haven't done it already, set up a separate savings account for each dream savings account that you identified on your worksheet. (Special accounts like a college 529 or a dedicated Health Savings Account will be housed outside of your bank.) Once the accounts are set up, you will have a series of auto transfers moving money on specifically chosen days. Do not worry. You will get used to the timing and flows of your money into these various accounts. Your bank should have an easy way of automating all transfers each week from your master checking to your various savings accounts, and you can also set up these transfers online yourself.

Olivia's New Financial Path

Olivia had the college experience of a lifetime at a top-notch, private liberal arts school. The journey of college and career began when she got her offer letter for the college covering half of tuition and room and board, but not the rest. Olivia and her parents had to make a big decision. Their savings still left about $12,000 per year that they couldn't pay, and they made the decision to use student loans to cover it.

Olivia then landed a great job making $45,000 in marketing at a manufacturing company. Her years and efforts of networking and internships paid off. She was by far the highest-paid graduate of her peers.

Her first month on the job, Olivia came to talk to me—the advisor on her retirement plan—only we don't get to retirement for a while. She couldn't think or talk about anything other than that $50,000 in debt. She explained how she tried everything to keep her expenses down so that she could throw every last dollar at the debt, but it didn't seem to be making a dent.

We quickly got to work making a plan. Olivia came prepared with her expenses, which we threw into our cash planning model.

Though she winced at the thought of doing anything other than paying off her student loans, we began with our Pay Yourself First process. We got her salary info and plugged in 10%.

1. Pay Yourself First: Retirement Savings & Debt Reduction

Gross pay ($3,750) x __10__ % retirement savings and debt reduction rate

= __$375__

Take-home pay before investments __$2,563__

Pay Yourself First __− 375__

NET PAY = __$2,188__ / MONTH

Next, we chatted about what she might want to save for, from travel (her passion) to having the money to repair her car. She had originally wanted a new car, but after thinking and reflecting she realized that while living at home, she would be far better off getting a head start on other more important things to her. As we spoke, we crafted numbers around those goals and priorities. I asked her to consider saving into an emergency fund aggressively at $300 per month while living at home, both to avoid lifestyle creep and to also get a head start on the fund. Olivia really wanted to be able to get her own place in a year or two, so we put aside $300 per month for moving expenses, furnishings and deposit. She opted not to get the car and instead to save ahead for repairs and eventually buying her next car (hopefully after her loans were repaid). Olivia's company has a high deductible healthcare plan, so she opted to deposit $50 into the Health Savings Account (HSA) with the company. She also set up a gift budget for Christmas, birthdays, etc.

2. Save for Future Expenses
Automate Savings

Set up savings accounts earmarked for emergency fund and other expenses (i.e. home repairs, new car, vacation, gifts, etc.)

__Emergency__ : $ __300__ / month   __Healthcare__ : $ __50__

__Apartment__ : $ __300__   __Travel__ : $ __100__

Car Repair/Purchase : $ __50__   __Gifts & Charity__: $ __25__

Savings Total = $ __825__ / month

(Net Pay) - (Savings Total) = $ __1,363__ (A)

Next came bills. Olivia lived with her parents, so she didn't have a rent payment. She dreamed of a beautiful apartment in a hip part of the city, but it would cost $1,200. We put that decision on hold and filled in the other bills we could anticipate. We prioritized her student loan bill on a 20-year repayment, which came to $370 per month. We agreed that after her emergency fund was built, she could put additional payments toward the student loans every month. Also, she committed to future windfalls, tax refunds, and pay raises going toward her student loans. Her homework for the bills was to set up insurance, student loans, rent, and anything else she could put on autopay. This left a few items she would spend each month that were variable and thus cut down on a lot of financial "work" she would have to do each month. Here was her bills budget:

3. Pay Fixed Expenses

Automate payments for fixed expenses, (i.e. rent/mortgage, utilities, cell phone, internet, minimum payments for credit cards & other debt)

Mortgage/Rent : $ __0__ / month   Cell Phone : $ __50__

__utilities__ : $ __150__   Insurance : $ __65__

__Internet__ : $ __40__   Student Loans : $ __370__

__TV__ : $ __35__   Netflix : $ __10__

Total = $ __720__ / month

(A) - (Fixed Expenses) = $ __643__ (B)

This left her with $643 per month, or $148 per week to "spend." Olivia really wasn't sure about this one. Would it be enough? Would she run out of money? I reassured her that if that was the case, we could always go back to the bills and savings accounts to make cuts that would allow more money to drop down to Step 4. The only problem would be that those cuts would impact student loans or her precious savings accounts. We estimated what her weekly spending needs were and realized that it could have a chance of working.

4. Spend the Rest

THINK: ALL OTHER EXPENSES, (i.e. gas, groceries, dining out, Netflix, clothes)

Option 1: Spend the rest (B) in your account down to zero each month.

Option 2: Go the extra mile! Open a second checking account and spend weekly:

Take (B) x 12 = $ __7,716__ (C)

Divide (C) ÷ 52 = $ __148__

Move this amount of money over each week into the second checking account and spend down to zero with a debit card.

Spend the rest (weekly)	$148
Food	– $60
Home Supplies	– $10
Fuel	– $20
Clothing	– $25
Hair/Beauty	– $20
Entertainment	– $13
	= 0

The Big Picture

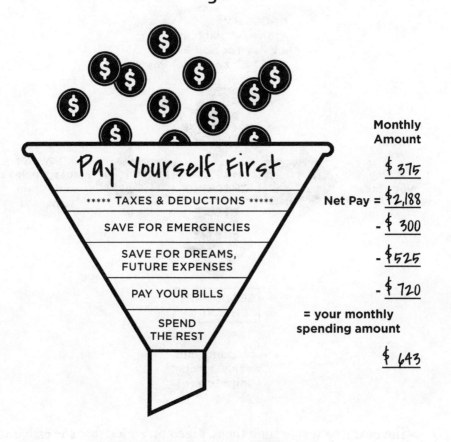

	Monthly Amount
Pay Yourself First	$ 375
***** TAXES & DEDUCTIONS *****	Net Pay = $2,188
SAVE FOR EMERGENCIES	- $ 300
SAVE FOR DREAMS, FUTURE EXPENSES	- $525
PAY YOUR BILLS	- $ 720
SPEND THE REST	= your monthly spending amount $ 643

Where does your money go?	
Taxes	25.0%
Healthcare/Pre-Tax Withholdings	6.7%
1. Pay Yourself First	10.0%
2. Save for Future Expenses	22.0%
3. Pay Your Bills	19.2%
4. Spend the Rest	17.1%

Olivia did her homework first, which was to set up all her savings accounts. In the end, she had six savings accounts and one additional checking account since she already had her master checking account set up.

Here was the map of Olivia's money when we were finished:

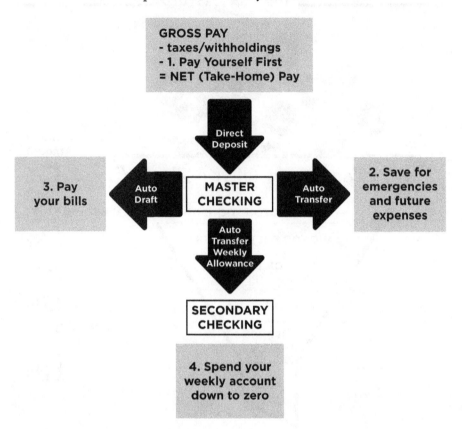

The next step was to fund them. I recommended that she ease into her savings accounts over a three-month period. This way, cash would naturally build up in her checking account to create a natural buffer, and she would not run the risk of something coming up that she had not accounted for.

We settled on funding the emergency fund ($300) and gift account ($25) first, so she set up an auto draft into each account out of her master checking account. She scheduled those to happen monthly on the 15th to coincide with her second paycheck since her bills hit on her first paycheck.

Next, she set up her weekly spending account at her bank, which was a checking account. She also requested a debit account for it. Olivia said funding on Monday would work best for her because, like a lot of people, she would have the incentive to spend as little as possible early in the week. Then she could have a little more fun on the weekend. Olivia set up an auto transfer from her master checking account to her spending account for $148 to happen weekly, starting the following Monday.

I asked Olivia to think of something she would do that would be fun/frivolous/indulgent if she had money leftover in her spending account at the end of the week. She settled on transferring that money to her travel account.

And then we waited to see how it would work.

The great thing about this system is that its ability to work hinges largely on whether the weekly spending works. It's an immediate indicator if you have an unrealistic budget. Olivia's job was to test out that weekly amount.

To my delight, Olivia reported that her weekly spend was plenty. She still had $25 left over on Sunday that she allowed to trickle into the next week. Apparently, it was a lot of fun to figure out all the ways she could NOT spend, something that she never used to do because the money just disappeared every month. But before this system, there was never an incentive for her.

We then tested the budget for a month. The bills came out the first of the month, she got her weekly transfers, and then the second half of the month, her two savings transfers happened. At the end of the month, she went through her master account to see if there was anything related to her new savings accounts (emergency and gifts). Sure enough, when she went through her credit card statement, most of the items were bills, but she had bought a $10 Starbucks gift card for a friend that month. So, she transferred $10 from her gift account into her master checking account and then paid her credit card bill.

As expected from our calculation, she ended the month with an extra $500, from the savings transfers she *didn't* make for her dream apartment, car repairs, travel, and healthcare.

The next month, Olivia added her home apartment draft to the 15th of the month in the amount of $300, and then by month four she transferred $50 for car repairs, $50 for healthcare, and $100 for travel.

By month four, Olivia had the routine of reconciling her credit card and master checking account spending for any expenses that were not bills and would therefore need to be reimbursed by any savings accounts. She said there were a couple weeks where she spent her weekly account to zero by Saturday and had to eat ramen noodles on Sunday, but for the most part she never minded it. The other weeks she could routinely transfer money to the travel account, and before she even knew it that account had $400 in it—$300 from regular monthly transfers and an extra $100 from all the small weekly deposits.

Most of all, what Olivia loved was the sense of security she felt from knowing she was saving for retirement. She said it was funny that even though retirement was not a passion, knowing that money was piling up somewhere made her feel good. The emergency fund provided a similar sense of comfort.

He Said "Yes" (to The System)

At 28, Olivia had her pile of cash, a dwindling student loan balance down to $47,000 from $50,000, and an apartment of her own at $700 per month. Sure, it was not the apartment she had originally dreamed of, but being able to move out on her own last year was exciting.

And just last week, the man of her dreams, Adam, asked her to marry him. She said "yes." But a week later, she had a question for him. "Will you use my cash flow system?" It was their first conversation on money, and Olivia knew that getting on the right foot with money immediately was critical to keeping finances from being a problem down the road in their marriage. She walked Adam through her budget that she kept on a crinkled and marked up piece of paper and then opened up her bank account to show him the system of transfers. He was able to see the vision for their finances together.

Adam got excited, and he pulled up a spreadsheet. He added their combined income at the top. At the time he was only saving 5% to max out his company match, but Olivia had insisted that he increase that to 10%. It made sense to him, so he calculated that savings rate into his own income.

Adam made $50,000 in his logistics job for a trucking company. His only debt was a car payment of $400 per month, finally ending in 6 months.

They were worried about the cost of the wedding, but with a candid conversation with each set of parents, found out that they had planned to pay for the wedding. Olivia and Adam vowed to stay under the $10,000 budget to keep their finances moving in the right direction.

A year later, they married, and it was time to officially implement the budget. Olivia was thrilled. She knew how to control and direct money according to her dreams and joy. Now, with a combined household income of more than double her own, she and Adam had the ability to save first for retirement, and from there save for the down-payment on their first home, give to their church and other charitable organizations, to travel more extensively, and to spend the next year saving and preparing their finances for eventually having kids.

While a combined salary of $95,000 seemed like so much money, Adam and Olivia knew that having children would strain their budget if they weren't careful. Daycare alone costs $700 per month on average in their town. So they made a significant decision. They decided to move into Olivia's apartment to keep their overhead down and expenses fixed. That way, they could save aggressively for a down payment on a home and for the deductible that they would have to pay if they had a baby.

The conversation on student loans was the most important one. At the rate Olivia was paying on her loans, she would have them for a long time. Playing with numbers, they realized they could pay an extra 4%

of their combined gross income toward the student loans, or $317 per month. Then by putting every last windfall, like pay increases and tax refunds, towards the debt, it would be paid off in seven years or less. Just running those numbers, knowing the plan to get out from under that debt, gave Olivia a lightness she hadn't felt since she first came to grips with the debt.

This was a two-year plan. And these two lovebirds delighted in their start in life. They felt anchored by the savings that they got to see piling up. They loved the open and free communication about money that neither had experienced in their households growing up.

They were passionate about giving to their church and other charitable causes, and they wanted to give 10% of their money in this way. That would be $791 per month, and it became clear it wasn't going to work until her student loans were repaid. They settled on $100 per month but knew their goal was going to be to work their way to 10% over time on tithing.

Here was how things shaped up. (These are rounded, approximate numbers for the sake of simplicity.)

They both increased their savings to 10% and then took 4% of their combined gross pay in extra student loan payments, changing their take-home pay to $4,113.

Gross Monthly Pay	$7,917
Taxes	-$1,979
Healthcare/Pre-Tax Withholdings	-$717
Take-Home Pay Before Investments	$5,221
Pay Yourself First	-$1,109

1. Pay Yourself First: Retirement Savings & Debt Reduction

Gross pay (**$7,917**) x __10__ % retirement savings and 4% debt reduction rate

$$= \underline{\$792 + \$317} =$$

$$\underline{\$1,109}$$

Take-Home Pay Before Investments	**$5,221**
Pay Yourself First	**-$1,109**

NET PAY = $4,113* / MONTH

*rounded, approximate numbers

They settled on a lot of savings accounts since they had several areas to defend against, including the other car breaking down and needing expensive repairs, the healthcare cost of hitting a $3,000 deductible to have a baby, one of them temporarily losing a job, and the one-time expense of their annual charitable giving. They were most excited about starting the travel account.

A walk-away fund, in the event that one of them lost or needed to leave their job, was established with a high interest savings account, and they set up a payroll deduction straight into that account for $300 per month out of their paychecks. It was important to them that they never see the money, so they would never be tempted to rob it. They knew that it would be difficult to save aggressively for emergencies once they had to pay a daycare bill, so they decided to front load that account and drop it down to $50–$100 after they had a child. The rest of the money for daycare would come after the car payment went away and could be redirected for that purpose.

Next, they went to their bank and set up a "downpayment"" account, as well as accounts for "car repair," "travel," and "gifts and charity," establishing auto transfers into those accounts on the 15th of the month to allow both paychecks to arrive in their accounts prior to the money being drafted.

Finally, Adam set up a health savings account with his company that they used for insurance, and he arranged to have $100 payroll deducted into the Healthcare HSA.

2. Save for Future Expenses
Automate Savings

Set up savings accounts earmarked for emergency fund and other expenses (i.e. home repairs, new car, vacation, gifts, etc.)

Walk-Away Fund : $ 300 / month   Healthcare : $ 100

Down Payment : $ 125   Travel : $ 150

Car Repair/Purchase : $ 100   Gifts & Charity : $ 150

Savings Total = $ 925 / month

(Net Pay) - (Savings Total) = $ 3,188 (A)

Bills were a source of stress, even with a relatively low rent. They had a lot of fixed overhead for what they made and probably would for a while while they had the minimum student loan payments that had to be made and the inevitable day care that would replace the car payment eventually. But both of them knew this was a temporary state. They committed to spending their energy on finances, finding ways to lower payments, and increase what would bring happiness as a family: travel and experiences.

3. Pay Fixed Expenses

Automate payments for fixed expenses, (i.e. rent/mortgage, utilities, cell phone, internet, minimum payments for credit cards & other debt)

Mortgage/rent : $ __700__ / month   _Insurance_ : $ __120__

Utilities : $ __300__   _Car Payment_ : $ __400__

Internet : $ __70__   _Life Insurance_ : $ __40__

Cable : $ __60__   _Student Loans_ : $ __370__

Cell Phone : $ __150__

Total = $ __2,210__ / month

(A) - (Fixed Expenses) = $ __977__ (B)

Finally, what was left over was really not very much. They were lucky to have this system for the use of the second checking account because they could easily go over budget on spending. They would only have $977 per month to spend on everything else, which translated to $226 per week. They figured if they were careful throughout the week that they would have enough for a weekly date night at a restaurant.

Here is the spending budget they came up with:

4. Spend the Rest

THINK: ALL OTHER EXPENSES, (i.e. gas, groceries, dining out, Netflix, clothes)

Option 1: Spend the rest (B) in your account down to zero each month.

Option 2: Go the extra mile! Open a second checking account and spend weekly:

Take (B) x 12 = $ __11,730__ (C)

(C) ÷ 52 = $ __226__

Move this amount of money over each week into the second checking account and spend down to zero with a debit card.

The Big Picture

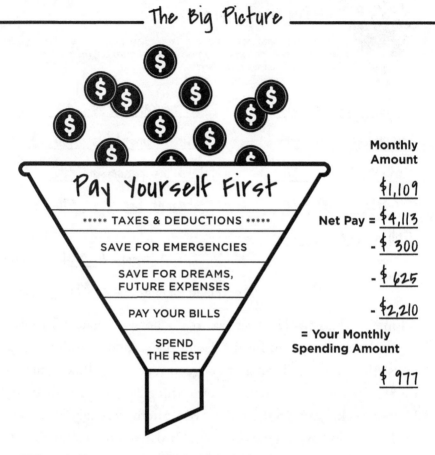

	Monthly Amount
Pay Yourself First	$1,109
***** TAXES & DEDUCTIONS *****	Net Pay = $4,113
SAVE FOR EMERGENCIES	- $300
SAVE FOR DREAMS, FUTURE EXPENSES	- $625
PAY YOUR BILLS	- $2,210
SPEND THE REST	= Your Monthly Spending Amount
	$977

When bills get out of whack, stress goes up. Even with very low rent, look at how bills were eating away at their budget: 27.9%!

Where does your money go?	
Taxes	25.0%
Healthcare/pre-tax withholdings	9.1%
1. Pay Yourself First	14.0%
2. Save for Future Expenses	11.7%
3. Pay Your Bills	27.9%
4. Spend the Rest	12.3%

Imagine if they had done what most couples do, NOT budgeted, and instead did the first thing every young married couple wants to do: Buy a home! The banks would have approved them for a $300,000 home. With no downpayment, they would have to pay mortgage insurance until they had built enough equity, or ownership, in the home to equal 20%. The total payment with property taxes and insurance would come to $1,800! Look how tight their budget is with a rent payment of $700 per month. Imagine the sacrifices they would have to make to afford that payment month after month—the sacrifices to their happiness.

Olivia and Adam are a rare couple that not only started out their lifelong marital journey in love but also in financial stability. This is all a credit to Olivia learning, internalizing, and then sharing her cash management system. Olivia may not look exactly like you, but I hope you can benefit from seeing the system put to work through the lens of her life, and join me in cheering her on.

YOU CAN DO THIS

The ultimate freedom is the ability to walk away from work one day into a retirement of your own dreams—whatever that may look like. But the in-between—the life you will live, God-willing, between now and retirement—is the essence of this cash management system. Don't worry about the money transfers and the names of accounts and whether the credit card or debit card is the right system. The logistics are easy. The results are profound.

I believe true freedom can only come from living below your means and building a pile of cash so you can live the life that you dream of. This is not a choice among many choices as to how you live your life. It is a binary one. Will you live a life of freedom or will you not? It may seem that people live pretty good lives on the edge with no safety net and with debt of many kinds from mortgages to cars to credit cards. Do not be fooled. They are owned and governed by their financial situation. They don't dare listen to their heart's longing to pursue another career path, start that business, take a year-long sabbatical, go back to school, or work part-time while they write a book. They just wake up every morning, go to work, and do it all over again the next day.

Entrepreneurship has been declining for decades. Why? When we live paycheck to paycheck or payment to payment, we don't dare to dream.

If you have debt of any kind, my best wisdom to you is to get uncomfortable and remain at a level of discomfort with that debt. Imagine it gone. Set the date for when it will be gone. Make a plan for it to go away. Direct your first dollars (after retirement savings) toward that debt. I believe that the biggest problem with debt is the peculiar comfort we have with it as a society.

Money isn't everything. The obsession with it can hamper or devalue human connection. Money sure is a lot, though, especially when it is still the only currency to buy time, opportunity, and generosity. It offers the freedom to be who you want to be, how you want to be, and where you want to be. Isn't that all we can want in life?

I saw Olivia as a young person failed by our system. Before she even had a fully formed prefrontal cortex, she took on crippling debt. That debt led to a choice right out of the gate that she never dreamed of—moving back in with her parents. Mentally, this manifested itself as resignation to a life of debt.

Maybe that's not you. You don't have student loan debt, and you successfully moved out on your own at 22. What a gift. You get to start out life without that hanging over you, and with a lifelong cash management system right out of the gate, you can build up your pile, or multiple piles, of cash.

Expect to pay your dues. Take the jobs you can get. Work your behind off. None of that would be much different from most . . . with one exception. As your cash piles up, you'll be watching your dreams inevitably pile up along with it. Maybe that pile of money will give you confidence to ask for that promotion and pay raise, put pen to paper for a business plan on that "crazy" idea, take that entire month off to finally backpack in Thailand, drop everything to volunteer after a natural disaster, or go to college or graduate school. Saving a little each month will become routine, but the soaring feeling of having that savings will never feel routine. It will serve as your constant reminder that you are free to live the life you were born for, the life you intend to live.

Finally, remember that this never was and never will be about deprivation. I want you to have the ability to buy the things and experiences that will bring you joy in your life.

But first, I want you to Save 10.

You're Invited to Join the Save10 Movement

As a way to support your efforts, I encourage you to join Save10. It is a movement to encourage women aged 18 to 30 to commit to saving 10% for retirement. You can make the commitment at Save10challenge.com. Be counted as a saver in the movement.

You can also join our women-only, private Facebook group called Save10, where thousands of women talk about money all day long. They share tips, ask questions, and celebrate savings and debt repayment victories. Many women have reported that with the support of the group they have taken brave financial steps to reverse their direction along difficult financial paths.

The Save10 movement is housed with the Women's Foundation of Arkansas, which supports our financial needs. We avoid conflicts of interest this way, meaning we want to make sure that no one can "sell" potentially harmful products to people in the group. Instead, it is driven by mutual support and guided by informed, non-conflicted expertise.

We have simple goals: Save 10%, build an emergency fund, and pay off debt.

Please join us. We need your voice.

Your purchase of this book has supported the movement, as 10% of author royalties will support the work of Save10.

SOURCES, RESOURCES, & TOOLS

I want to welcome you to the exciting life of saving and financial independence. Know that this book is the product of standing on the shoulders of many giants who have studied the brain and/or applied those studies to money. My hope is that you can follow the trail of breadcrumbs via notes and tools below, and discover people and resources that can further the journey we just began.

My website dedicated to this book is **ButFirstSave10.com**. It will host further reading and resources on many of the topics discussed. Importantly, the website has worksheets to implement your own pay yourself first cash management system along with video tutorials on how to use them.

If you want to follow my own work in this money space, I encourage you to subscribe to my mailing list at **ladysplainingmoney.com** to stay up to date on publications and new resources. There is nothing like the ongoing conversation we are having on the following social media platforms:

- /LadysplainingMoney, /Save10, and /AptusFinancial
- /Ladysplaining.Money
- @LadysplainingM

INTRODUCTION

1. Zweig, Jason. *Your Money and Your Brain: How the New Science of Neuroeconomics Can Help Make You Rich.* Simon & Schuster, 2008. p. 265.

2. Collins, JL. *The Simple Path to Wealth: Your Road Map to Financial Independence and a Rich, Free Life.* Self-published, CreateSpace, 2016. p. 2

SPENDER OR SAVER: HOW WILL YOU WRITE YOUR LIFE STORY?

3. Robin, Vicki, and Dominguez, Joe. *Your Money or Your Life: 9*

Steps to Transforming Your Relationship with Money and Achieving Financial Independence. Revised ed., Penguin, 2018. p. 54.

4. Haidt, Jonathan. *The Happiness Hypothesis: Finding Modern Truth in Ancient Wisdom*. Basic Books, 2006. p. 84.

5. Robin, Vicki, and Dominguez, Joe. *Your Money or Your Life: 9 Steps to Transforming Your Relationship with Money and Achieving Financial Independence*. Revised ed., Penguin, 2018. p. 18.

6. Clements, Jonathan. *How to Think About Money*. Self-published, CreateSpace, 2016. p. 70.

THE INSPIRATION: PAY YOURSELF FIRST AND SAVE 10

7. "Farnoosh Torabi: How to Feel in Control of Your Money." *Stay Grounded with Raj Jana*, episode 65. *Apple Podcasts*, 24 February 2019.

8. "Farnoosh Torabi: How to Feel in Control of Your Money." *Stay Grounded with Raj Jana*, episode 65. *Apple Podcasts*, 24 February 2019.

9. Bessette, Linda. *Mindful Money: A Path to Simple Finances*. Bird Call Press, 2014. p. 57.

10. Thaler, Richard H., and Sunstein, Cass R. *Nudge: Improving Decisions About Health, Wealth, and Happiness*. Revised ed., Penguin, 2009. p. 107

11. Pant, Paula. "How to 'Afford Anything.'" *YouTube*, uploaded by Talks at Google, 18 March 2019, https://www.youtube.com/watch?v=awuTbPVCSH4&feature=emb_title

12. Krygowski, B.C. *Spending Habits for Professionals Who Want to FIRE*. Self-published, FIRE Freedom Press, 2019. p. 15.

The Millionaire Next Door: The Surprising Secrets of America's Wealthy by William Danko and Thomas Stanley (Longstreet, 1996) was an important piece in my own life. On the road to finding financial independence, an aspirational side of me had to die—the side that cared whether people thought I was rich or successful. This book has changed many lives by helping us understand that wealth doesn't look like we think it does. A great follow up book was co-authored by Thomas Stanley and his daughter, Sarah Fallaw, called *The Next Millionaire Next Door: Enduring Strategies for Building Wealth* (Lyons, 2018). Fallaw takes many of the same concepts and expands on them with her own research and application for a modern era.

I Will Teach You to Be Rich by Ramit Sethi (Workman, 2009) is a relatable book for young people that should be on a reading list. My team at Aptus has read this book and recommends it. The edgy straight talk is wildly effective at getting personal finance ideas packaged in a way that we can understand and act on them.

The financial independence movement came out of the 2008/2009 crisis and grew a generation of (mostly) young people eager to get off that hedonic treadmill and design their own lives. While people have vastly differing definitions of their FI motivations and goals, they all have one thing in common: super high savings rates. (Like 30%–40%, compared to the meager 10% that I am recommending in this book.) If this is your first personal finance book, and it is inspiring to you, then immerse yourself in the podcast, book, documentary, and blog of ChooseFI. Jonathan Mendonsa and Brad Barrett are giving space for FI curious people, hopefully like yourself, to constellate.

THE PERSPIRATION
13. Turner, James D. *The Physician Philosopher's Guide to Personal Finance: The 20% of Personal Finance Doctors Need to Know to Get 80% of the Results.* The Physician Philosopher, 2019. p. 140.

WOMEN WILL LEAD US OUT OF THIS SAVINGS CRISIS
14. Munnel, Alicia H., et al. *Women, Marriage, and the National Retirement Risk Index.* Trustees of Boston College, Center for Retirement Research, 2019. p. 3. https://crr.bc.edu/wp-content/uploads/2019/06/IB_19-10.pdf
15. "CFP Professional Demographics." *CFP Board.*
16. Jaekel, Astrid, and St-Onge, Elizabeth. "Why Women Aren't Making It to the Top of Financial Services Firms." *Harvard Business Review.* October 2016. https://hbr.org/2016/10/why-women-arent-making-it-to-the-top-of-financial-services-firms\
17. Thaler, Richard H., and Sunstein, Cass R. *Nudge: Improving Decisions About Health, Wealth, and Happiness.* Revised ed., Penguin, 2009. p. 110.
18. Anderson, Drew M., and Collins, Michael J. "Can Knowledge

Empower Women to Save More for Retirement?" *Center for Retirement Research at Boston College*, 2017. p. 3. https://crr.bc.edu/wp-content/uploads/2017/09/wp_2017-12.pdf. Working paper.

19. Bucher-Koenen, Tabea, et al. "How Financially Literate Are Women? An Overview and New Insights." *Global Financial Literacy Excellence Center*, 2016. https://gflec.org/wp-content/uploads/2016/02/WP-2016-1-How-Financially-Literate-Are-Women.pdf?x70028. Working paper.

20. Duke, Annie. *Thinking in Bets: Making Smarter Decisions When You Don't Have All the Facts.* Portfolio, 2018. p. 27.

21. Duke, Annie. *Thinking in Bets.* Portfolio, 2018. p. 28.

22. Collins, JL. *The Simple Path to Wealth: Your Road Map to Financial Independence and a Rich, Free Life.* Self-published, CreateSpace, 2016. p. 74.

23. Ellis, Charles D. "The Loser's Game." *Financial Analysts Journal*, vol. 51, no. 1, 1995.

SEE ALSO
2005 Letter to Shareholders of Berkshire Hathaway, Inc. Warren Buffet's Letters to Berkshire Shareholders, *Berkshire Hathaway, Inc.* https://www.berkshirehathaway.com/letters/2005ltr.pdf. p. 20.

24. Kumar, Alok. "Self-Selection and the Forecasting Abilities of Female Equity Analysts." *Journal of Accounting Research*, vol. 42, no. 2, 2010, pp. 394-397.

25. Barber, Brad, and Odean, Terrance. "Boys Will Be Boys: Gender, Overconfidence and Common Stock Investment." *Quarterly Journal of Economics.* February 2011. pp. 261–262.

26. Liu, Berlinda, and Brzenk, Phillip. *SPIVA® U.S. Scorecard Mid-Year 2019.* S&P Dow Jones Indices. p. 4.

27. "Who's the Better Investor, Men or Women?" *Fidelity*. 18 May 2017. https://www.fidelity.com/about-fidelity/individual-investing/better-investor-men-or-women

ADDITIONAL SOURCES
"Are Women Better Investors? Stash Data Flips Gender Stereotypes." *StashLearn*, Stash. 6 September 2018. https://learn.stashinvest.com/are-women-better-investors

Stewart, Neil. "Are women better investors than men?" *WBS News*,

Warwick Business School. 28 June 2018.

28. "Winning Over Women in Financial Services." *Kantar*, 2018. p. 9. https://us.kantar.com/media/1900352/winningoverwomen_report_fin. pdf

29. Anderson, Drew M., and Collins, Michael J. "Can Knowledge Empower Women to Save More for Retirement?" *Center for Retirement Research at Boston College*, 2017. p. 3.

THE FINANCIAL INDUSTRY

30. Thaler, Richard H., and Sunstein, Cass R. *Nudge: Improving Decisions About Health, Wealth, and Happiness*. Revised ed., Penguin, 2009. p. 271.

STEP 1: PAY YOURSELF FIRST

31. Thaler, Richard H., and Sunstein, Cass R. *Nudge: Improving Decisions About Health, Wealth, and Happiness*. Revised ed., Penguin, 2009. p. 113.

32. "What can you do to improve your finances in 2020?" *CNN*, 29 December 2019. https://www.cnn.com/videos/business/2019/12/29/managing-debt-financial-new-years-resolution-michelle-singletary-intv-ndwknd-vpx.cnn

33. "Farnoosh Torabi: How to Feel in Control of Your Money." *Stay Grounded with Raj Jana*, episode 65. *Apple Podcasts*, 24 February 2019.

34. "Retirement Income Calculator." *Vanguard*, The Vanguard Group. https://retirementplans.vanguard.com/VGApp/pe/pubeducation/calculators/RetirementIncomeCalc.jsf

35. "Social Security Quick Calculator." *The United States Social Security Administration*. https://www.ssa.gov/OACT/quickcalc/

36. Rutledge, Matthew S., et al. *Do Young Adults with Student Debt Save Less for Retirement?* Trustees of Boston College, Center for Retirement Research, 2018.

37. Robin, Vicki, and Dominguez, Joe. *Your Money or Your Life: 9 Steps to Transforming Your Relationship with Money and Achieving Financial Independence*. Revised ed., Penguin, 2018. p. 21.

We discuss student loans and the payment of them sparingly in this book. I could easily write a book solely focused on how to manage student loans. For a better understanding of student loans, be sure to check out blog posts, podcast episodes, and videos from Student Loan Planner, namely Travis Hornsby. All can be found at studentloanplanner.com. You can also see a link to Hornsby's talk at the EconoME conference in 2020 at ButFirstSave10.com.

National Public Radio's *Life Kit: Money* is a great podcast resource to find easily digestible financial information. The breadth of knowledge is wide and information is non-conflicted. This is a great stop for folks at the beginning of their personal finance journey.

For women entering high-income fields, I recommend exploring these offerings: Dr. Bonnie Koo, and her blog and podcast at wealthmommd.com; the blogs and podcast in The White Coat Investor network by The White Coat Investor, Dr. James Dahle; work by The Physician Philosopher, Dr. Jimmy Turner, including *The Physician Philosopher's Guide to Personal Finance and Investing* and the *Money Meets Medicine* podcast; and Physician on FIRE, Dr. Leif Dahleen. While these experts are primarily concerned with physicians, any high earners would share many of the same financial practices.

TOOLS
"Retirement Income Calculator." *Vanguard,* The Vanguard Group. https://retirementplans.vanguard.com/VGApp/pe/pubeducation/calculators/RetirementIncomeCalc.jsf

"Social Security Quick Calculator." *The United States Social Security Administration.* https://www.ssa.gov/OACT/quickcalc/

INVEST YOUR SAVINGS
38. Zweig, Jason. *Your Money and Your Brain: How the New Science of Neuroeconomics Can Help Make You Rich.* Simon & Schuster, 2008. p. 3.
39. Bogle, John C. *Enough: True Measures of Money, Business, and Life.* Revised ed., John Wiley & Sons, 2010. p. 80.
40. Bogle, John C. *The Little Book of Common Sense Investing: The Only Way to Guarantee Your Fair Share of Stock Market Returns.* 2nd ed., John Wiley & Sons, 2017. p. 111.

Thinking, Fast and Slow (Farrar, Straus and Giroux, 2011) by Daniel

Kahneman (winner of the Nobel Prize in Economics) is bedrock to understanding the functions of the two sides of the brain. It is applicable to many areas of money and finance, but I think in more dramatic ways helps us understand our investing brain.

I recommend reading Jason Zweig's column, *The Intelligent Investor*, in *The Wall Street Journal*. He has a deep understanding of behavioral economics and of the world of finance. He takes current financial events and helps us understand the brain. For a great sampling (and one of my favorites) check out this piece on hindsight bias: Zweig, Jason. "The Panic of 2020? Oh, I Made a Ton of Money—and So Did You." *The Wall Street Journal*, 20 March 2020. https://www.wsj.com/articles/the-panic-of-2020-oh-i-made-a-ton-of-moneyand-so-did-you-11584716442

John C. ("Jack") Bogle is considered a hero to many people, me included, and I recommend anything he's written for an understanding of passive mutual fund investing. I usually recommend people new to DIY investing read *The Little Book of Common Sense Investing: The Only Way to Guarantee Your Fair Share of Stock Market Returns* (Wiley, 2007).

STEP 2: PAY FOR FUTURE EXPENSES
41. Gabler, Neal. "The Secret Shame of Middle-Class Americans." *The Atlantic*, May 2016. https://www.theatlantic.com/magazine/archive/2016/05/my-secret-shame/476415/

TOOLS
Paycheck net-pay calculator: https://www.calculator.net/take-home-pay-calculator.html

STEP 3: PAY YOUR BILLS

42. Dahle, James M. *The White Coat Investor: A Doctor's Guide to Personal Finance and Investing*. White Coat Investor, 2014. p. 50.

TOOLS
College fund savings calculator for parents, grandparents, and others wishing to contribute: tools.finra.org/college_savings/

ACKNOWLEDGMENTS

But last, thank you . . .

Jorge, there would be no book without you, my forever salsa dancing partner, constantly listening and learning engineer, avid reader, fútbol aficionado, and my biggest cheerleader. When I would put the book down for long stretches, you encouraged me to pick it back up.

This book was a three-year process. It started at a hotel in Miami over a New Year's vacation with your family. Every morning, you held down the fort with a newborn and two small children under five years old so that I could head down to the hotel lobby to write down all these thoughts in my head. But what was supposed to be a quick, one-month writing project ended up being a multi-year process with many more mornings working on this.

The inspiration for this book has been the process of living different lives than society has told us to live as a married couple. We each dream big, cherish, and work to make those dreams a reality. We are willing to sacrifice for each other's dreams. When I started my financial company, Aptus, we were newly married and sidestepped many comforts for something that had a likelihood to fail. Yet you never wavered. We lived on your salary for a long time until Aptus took off. The exit from the hedonic treadmill took time, but what we have found is true freedom to live the way we want and teach our kids to live lives marching by their own tune.

You are the silent type, so when you speak, we all listen intently. At the dinner table, amidst the chaos of our rowdy kiddos, you will occasionally come down from the dreamy palace of your brain and thoughts to mouth quietly, "We are so freaking lucky."

Yes, we are.

Speaking of kids, when I started this book, I had babies. Now, I have children. Marco, Max, and Lucia, there are no words to express my love and appreciation for you, my teachers. You fiercely defend the present, whether it's delight in a sprouting cucumber, rescuing a turtle, or "making together" at dinner. Each of you has inspired different elements of this book, and each of you at some point was sleeping on or next to me during the majority of the process, which mostly happened in the wee hours of the morning.

Overwhelming thanks to Linda Bessette, my financial teacher, mentor, friend, and fellow dreamer who accepted an invitation to meet at Starbucks and changed my life forever. In you, I met someone passionate about personal finance who dedicated her life to getting financial wisdom and financial solutions into the hands of people who needed it. You showed me the path to how financial advice could be delivered ethically—by simply letting people pay for it directly. You taught me kindness and empathy, not judgement, for people struggling with tough financial situations. Amazingly, you just *gave* it all to me. All the advice. All the training. A gift from mentor to mentee. As if that wasn't enough, you allowed me to pluck you out of a well-deserved retirement to jump onto the roller coaster of Aptus. Aptus is our loving achievement of everything we dreamed about over our lattes. This book is everything we care and dream about. There are sentences in it that I am not sure if I said or you said. I have sincere gratitude to you for writing and rewriting. Your patience and dedication are incalculable.

Erin Wood, when you shared the incredible news that Et Alia Press would publish *But First, Save 10*, little did I know that you were giving me the gift of the book I didn't dare to dream was possible. You guided our team of readers and editors through a process to put truths on a pedestal, whittle down the unnecessary, and speak in a language of love for the reader. You pushed me to work harder than I ever thought possible, but you were my own life buoy to pick up redrafts, tasks, and design decisions when I was overwhelmed. You gave countless hours of your time during every editing round. And this was necessary in hindsight. Money is too emotional, and readers deserve words, phrases, and sentences that are relatable, factual, and even poetic at times. Thank you for loving this book as much as I love it.

Stephanie Matthews, it all began in 2019 after I floated the idea to a group creating a movement of women saving 10%. You asked for a meeting and in your kind and direct way, nailed down the entire plan for Save10—for an audacious goal to get 10,000 women to commit to saving 10% for retirement. Then, you directed the execution to achieve that goal. You are savvy and knowledgeable about money, an incredible speaker and spokesperson, a creative marketer and diligent worker, and a tender, sweet friend to me and so many. How one person got to come to this earth with so many gifts and the willingness to share them with fellow humans baffles me. All I know is that I am incredibly grateful that you co-founded Save10 with me, joined the Et Alia team for *But First, Save10*, and joined the Aptus team to grow our vision to transform company retirement plans. I don't know how I deserve it, but I thank you for believing in me.

Amy Ashford's talented graphics and layout design simplified what used to be complex. She understood the mission of *But First, Save10* and used images and happy, clean, beautiful fonts to make saving visually appealing.

I have so much gratitude to the team of Et Alia editors: Lindsey Fisher, Kaitlin Lowe, Victoria Mays, Emma Lassiter, and Angela Dribben. They continuously challenged ideas with thought provoking questions, suggestions, and edits.

I am so thankful for the readers, including Ryder Buttry, Kate Pendergast, Lizzie Phillips, Linda Bessette, Audrey Li, and Tim Quillin.

My Aptus family is the reason there is a company that has successfully shown the world that financial advice can be delivered in a way that is accessible to most people and without conflicts of interest. Tim Quillin, you took a leap of incredible faith when you joined Aptus early on. You believed in the Aptus virtues and then set us on the course to grow a company that would have a national reach. Thank you for being a steadying force to keep us on the trajectory to impact so many lives and for creating our unifying Aptus financial planning process.

Matt Duncan, what a gift you are to me and to clients. No one can sniff out a rogue figure, dig down into numbers deeper, and get to the truth for clients better. Mary Tellez, we have learned that true empathy, understanding, and love can change people's financial lives. You have shown us that and shown me that one can "Brené Brown" their life and the lives of others to make us all better. And to the clients and retirement plan participants for your stories of overcoming incredible financial hardships or getting out of tough patterns, this book is the one that you said you wished someone gave you. I hope I did it justice.

My parents, Jim and Susan, married 44 years, sacrificed so much for my education and grounded me in faith and family. Thank you for letting me experience money growing up, from the boring payments of bills to the exciting world of eagerly tracking stock ticker symbols in the paper. Who knew that it could unlock a future passion. And to my sister, Lizzie, a true saver. I learned from you early on the power of cash (you always had it) and the restraint required to build that cash over time. You were the one who first introduced me to the research and application of behavioral finance which now is the bedrock to Aptus and the concepts taught in this book. I thank my grandmother who taught me frugality (why pay more for something when you can pay less?) and who always encouraged me to write and speak when possible. To Warren and Harriet, thank you for lighting the path to thinking bigger and being bolder.

When I got married, I had no idea that instantly I would get a new sister, brother, parents, nephews and nieces, and more aunts and uncles than I can count. You all embraced me as your own, and while we all may not speak the same language, our mismatched words, laughter, dancing, and paella are special instruments to purvey our mutual love.

Cuando me casé, no tenía idea de que instantáneamente obtendría una nueva hermana, hermano, padres, sobrinos(as), y más tíos(as) de los que puedo contar. Todos ustedes me acogieron como si fuera unos de los suyos. Aunque no todos hablemos el mismo idioma, nuestras palabras mal dichas, las risas, bailes y paella son nuestros instrumentos especiales para alimentar nuestro amor mutuo.

To you all and my own aunts, uncles, and cousins—your platform of love gives me the grounding in "enough" and the courage to speak my truths. Your enduring love is all that matters.

To my gal pals, you are my oxygen, and I thank you for that. In the end, monthly dinner clubs, long walks, sharing funny memes, and being witness to the joys of births, life moments, and the pain of our losses is really all that matters in this life.

My high school years at Mount St. Mary Academy introduced me to the work of the amazing Sisters of Mercy and sowed seeds of social justice, compassion, and empathy. I am grateful to that grounding and the subsequent years at Salem College that were incredibly formative.

Finally, I want to express sincere gratitude to the Save10 community—Women's Foundation of Arkansas, leaders and supporters, those who trust the group with their vulnerable questions and commitments, and those who bravely save in a world of consumption. I especially thank those who have found financial success and are stretching out their hands to pull up women to join them.

Retirement Dreams

_____

_____

_____

_____

_____

_____

_____

_____

_____

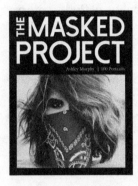

The Masked Project presents 100 portraits taken by photographer Ashley Murphy during the spring 2020 surge of COVID-19. From behind cotton and polypropylene, stars and grommets, leather and paisley, feathers and studs, eyes unmask worlds about personhood and pandemic life. The collection and flash reflections from Murphy's brief portrait sessions are moving reminders that alongside fears of the unknown stand our refusal to shrink and our unrelenting drive for self-expression. From a safe distance, we emerge bold and brave, known and remembered. *Forthcoming Fall 2020.*

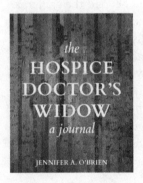

The raw, luminescent reflections of a caregiver-turned-widow chronicle the period following the diagnosis of her hospice doctor husband with advanced, metastatic cancer. O'Brien's art journal will help those facing death gain insight on how to live presently in dark hours, honor grief, and discover-even after devastating loss-ways to forge forward. Featured in the Six Bridges Book Festival and the Examined Life Conference. 8 x 10 premium color hardback. 86 pages. *$32.95.*

Meet fifty women—including a fire performer, a hatter, a kombucha brewer, and an aspiring time traveler—who will challenge the way you think about what it takes to lead a creative life. Let the failures, victories, and wisdom of these bold creatives help you step into creative freedom. Edited by Erin Wood. IPPY Silver Medal for Best Nonfiction South, INDIE Book Awards Finalist in Inspirational, Women's Issues, and Design categories, selected as a 2019 Arkansas Gem by Arkansas Center for the Book, and featured in the 2019 Arkansas Literary Festival. 8.5 x 11, standard color paperback with 250+ images. 200 pages. *$29.95.*

Explore concepts of art, history, and the feminine as you conjure the lives and habits of 20th century American women through the purses they carried. *What's Inside: A Century of Women and Handbags, 1900–1999* by Anita Davis compliments the permanent exhibition of ESSE Museum & Store, one of only three purse museums in the world. Featured in the Arkansas Literary Festival. 8.5 x 9 premium color paperback. 55+ images and illustrations. 118 pages. *$29.95.*

Can Everybody Swim? A Survival Story from Katrina's Superdome takes you beyond the camera's lens on a journey through the maelstrom. A fierce loyalty to protect the Gentilly neighborhood family home purchased by his Ecuadorian immigrant grandparents led the then twenty-five-year-old Bruce S. Snow and his family to remain in their City to weather the storm, including enduring six days in the infamous Superdome. IPPY Bronze Medalist. Featured in the Arkansas Literary Festival and Louisiana Book Festival. 252 pages. 6 x 9 standard color paperback. *$16.95.*

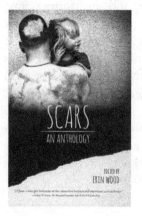

In *Scars: An Anthology*, edited by Erin Wood, forty contributors address self-mutilation, creating art, gender confirmation surgery, cancer, birth, brain injury, war, coming of age, pain, and love, all focusing on the central question of what it means to live with physical scars. Featured in the 2016 Arkansas Literary Festival, the Louisiana Book Festival, and Columbia University's Seminar in Narrative, Health, and Social Justice. 288 pages. 6 x 9 b&w paperback. 25+ images and illustrations. *$16.95.*